HOUSE TO HOUSE

HOUSE TO HOUSE

Larry Kreider

House To House Publications
1924 West Main Street • Ephrata, PA 17522

Many of the names used in this book have been changed to maintain privacy for the people mentioned. The personal illustrations and experiences used by the author are written from his personal viewpoint. Others who were involved, if given the opportunity, could add their point of view and provide a more complete account. There is full agreement, however, on the truth that God is building His church in our generation, and that all things work together for good to those who love God and are called according to His purpose.

DOVE Christian Fellowship International
1924 West Main Street, Ephrata, Pennsylvania 17522, U.S.A.
Telephone: 717-738-3751 or 800-848-5892
Fax: 717-738-0656
Email: dcfi@dcfi.org
Web site: www.dcfi.org

ISBN 1-880828-81-2

Unless otherwise noted, scripture quotations are taken from the New King James Version (NKJV) of the Holy Bible.
© 1979, 1980, 1982, Thomas Nelson Inc.

Printed in the United States of America

Dedication

". . . how I kept back nothing that was helpful, but proclaimed it to you, and taught you publicly and from **house to house,** *testifying to Jews, and also to Greeks, repentance toward God and faith toward our Lord Jesus Christ" (Acts 20:20-21).*

House to House is dedicated to my wife LaVerne, to our children Katrina, Charita, Joshua and Leticia, and to the hundreds of faithful cell group leaders and assistant leaders with whom we have had the privilege of serving during the past two decades.

Many of the spiritual principles outlined in this book were learned through the "School of the Holy Spirit." And we are still learning with each step of faith. Many believers have given of themselves to serve our Lord Jesus in the building of the "underground church" throughout the world. To them this book is also dedicated.

But most importantly of all, this book is dedicated to the One who has promised us that He will build His church . . . our Lord Jesus Christ.

Acknowledgments

Special thanks to Karen Ruiz for her overall editorial assistance, Sarah Mohler for layout and design, Hank Rogers for his oversight and assistance on this project, Jackie Bowser for writing the thought-provoking questions at the end of each chapter, Steve Prokopchak and Brian Sauder for helping me clearly communicate what the Lord has placed on my heart, Lee Grady for his editorial help, Ron Myer for "covering my tracks" to give me the time needed to write, and many others who proofread this book. To the dozens of people who read the manuscript and offered valuable insights every step of the way, "thank you."

And a very special thanks to those with whom we have been privileged to labor—the entire team, both at home and abroad, who have been so encouraging and supportive of my spending the time writing and rewriting this book.

CONTENTS

1. **What's an Underground Church?** 1
    Believers step out in faith to prepare flexible wineskins
2. **God's Priorities** 13
    The importance of prayer, evangelism and discipleship
3. **A Biblical Vision for Cell Groups** 19
    What was the early church really like?
4. **Spiritual Families** 31
    How we fit in as members of the Body
5. **Am I Qualified To Be A Cell Group Leader?** 41
    The kind of people God calls to leadership
6. **The Responsibilities of a Cell Group Leader** 57
    Cell leaders' and assistant cell leaders' responsibilities
7. **Leading Through Servanthood** 71
    The motivation of a servant-leader
8. **Reaching Out Beyond Ourselves** 85
    The basic purpose of meeting in small groups
9. **The Home Group Meetings** 105
    Flexibility and creativity—an important key
10. **Help! I'm a Cell Group Leader** 125
    Practical tips
11. **A Cell Leader's Commitment** 137
    Commitment to Jesus Christ and the church
12. **New Testament Church Leadership** 147
    The God-appointed leadership of apostles and elders
13. **Two Myths—Holy Men and Holy Buildings** 159
    Saints are called and equipped to minister
14. **Let's Dream Together** 169
    Preparing for the future

15. **Crossing the River** 177
    Pressing forward in the calling God gives to you
16. **Giving the Church Away** 183
    Update on DCFI and its transition to an apostolic network of cell-based churches
17. **Preparing for the Harvest** 193
    Working together to plant cells and churches

Appendix A: DCFI's Vision, Mission, Plan 197
Appendix B: DCFI's Values of the Kingdom 199
Notes 205
Index 208

FOREWORD

During this era of church life, the Holy Spirit is shifting the paradigms of God's people. It is astonishing to see the way old wineskins have started leaking and new ones have developed. Around the world, the Holy Spirit is forming cell churches. As He does so, His anointing is falling on chosen men. One of those men is Larry Kreider. When we first met, I was quickly aware that he had a mighty calling.

While there are many expressions of a cell church, the DOVE Christian Fellowship International model has many classic characteristics. First of all, it is primarily a *cell church* rather than a *church with cells*. The real paradigm shift takes place in ecclesiology when everything the people of God do is rooted exclusively in the life of the cell, not the large group. Another characteristic of the model expressed in this book is that it is a *movement*, not just a *parish*. Cell churches everywhere think globally, knowing that their ambassadors will all be "home grown" in the base church before being sent to plant new works.

Studies of people reveal that only 2.5% are *innovators*. Kreider is one of them. Innovators have the special capacity to see something as "real" when it is only theory, and then to make it come to pass. It is painful to have to backtrack and try another direction. This book is the result of many of those cycles. It can save the reader much time in experimentation.

Another major group of people, representing 13.5%, are *early adopters*. They are unable to accept something as possible until they actually see a working model. Once observed, they can repeat what they have seen. You, the reader, are most probably in this category. For you, Larry's book joins the small collection of writings that can steer you on your journey, and will be remembered as a pioneer's contribution to the family of God. Pick up a highlighter and begin to mark the pages which follow!

Dr. Ralph W. Neighbour, Jr.
Singapore, 1994

INTRODUCTION

New introduction for this updated edition of House to House:

It has been over thirty years since the Lord called my wife LaVerne and me into Christian leadership. In 1971, we helped start a youth ministry reaching out to unchurched kids in our community. From these seeds planted, the house to house strategy of DOVE Christian Fellowship International sprouted several years later. This book was originally written from the perspective of our experience with the new wineskins of cell groups in a cell-based church and our commitment to church planting throughout the nations.

New wineskins are continuing to emerge. Today, in addition to cell churches, new house churches and house church networks are growing throughout America and in the nations of the world. This new kind of wineskin especially appeals to Generation X, those 18-35 years of age. Like cell churches, house churches are relational and all members are liberated to serve as ministers. However, house churches are different in that each functions as a real church in a home complete with eldership. Cell churches, while meeting in homes during the week, are part of a larger unit—led by eldership at the congregational level. I firmly believe that we need many kinds of churches to fulfill the Great Commission. From traditional churches to cell-based churches to new house church networks—the Lord will use all types to help bring in the harvest during the last days.

The principles of cell group ministry in this book apply to training leaders for house churches as well as in cell-based congregations. I should also add that many of the new house churches springing up throughout the world have smaller cells within their house church for discipleship and leadership training. **This book can be used as a biblical manual to train cell leaders and house church leaders.** May the Lord use this book to equip you for His service during this strategic time in history. God bless you as together we prepare for the harvest!

Larry Kreider
October 2001

CHAPTER 1

WHAT'S AN
UNDERGROUND CHURCH?

A foreclosure on their house forced a young couple, Jack and Sue, to face the facts of Jack's alcohol problem. Hoping for a new start, they moved to south-central Pennsylvania from Long Island, New York. New to the community and feeling extremely lonely, one day Sue decided to take her nephew to a local park with hopes of making some new friends. Kathy, a young mother who serves with her husband as a cell group leader in our church, just happened to be in the park that day and struck up a conversation with Sue.

Sensing Sue's loneliness, Kathy invited her new friend to a get-together (cell meeting) at her home, to give her the opportunity to meet some more people in the community. They exchanged phone numbers and a few days later Kathy called Sue to remind her to come to their house the following Wednesday night. "Should we bring anything along to drink?" Sue asked.

"There's no need to bring anything along," Kathy said. "We are just going to sing a bit and then have a Bible study."

When she got off the phone, Sue looked at her husband and said, "Hey, whadda ya know— it's a bunch of holy rollers!" But the lady in the park was so nice that Sue and Jack both decided to go anyway. Jack liked the music, and they continued to go back. Within a few weeks, Sue received Jesus Christ. Jack was happy about the change that he saw in his wife, but he declined when he was also encouraged to receive Christ.

However, a few weeks later, Jack had an encounter with the Lord while at work. He was high up in a tree cutting off a branch when suddenly another falling branch hit him. It was a miracle he wasn't knocked to the ground. Knowing someone had to be watching over him, he cried out to the Lord and was genuinely converted. Today, Jack and Sue serve as cell group leaders in DOVE Christian Fellowship. Their story is just one of hundreds of stories that could be told of the lives we have seen the Lord change.

It all started during the summer of 1971, when my fiancee, LaVerne, and I helped to start a youth ministry with a small band of young people who began to reach out to the unchurched youth of our community in northern Lancaster County, Pennsylvania. We played sports and conducted various activities throughout the week for spiritually needy youngsters and teenagers. This kind of friendship evangelism produced results, and during the next few years, dozens of young people came to faith in Christ with a desire to be incorporated into a local church.

Every Sunday night we took van loads of these new believers to visit various churches in our community, because we wanted to help them find a local church. After the church services, the entire group usually returned to our home for a time of praise, prayer, spiritual counseling and just plain fun. Before long, some of the other leaders asked me to begin a weekly Bible study each Tuesday night for these new believers. Our desire was to teach them from the Scriptures what practical Christian living was really all about and assist them in being planted in a local church.

Those of us who served in this youth ministry were from various local churches, so we also attempted to help the new believers find their place in our local congregations. Although the Christians in the local churches were friendly and helpful, something wasn't clicking. These young believers simply were not being incorporated into the life of the established churches in our communities. Some of the believers from unchurched backgrounds were getting married and starting families of their own, but they were unable to feel at home within the church structures in our locale.

The Need for Flexible Wineskins

We began to understand the answer to our dilemma when a church leader shared the following verses from Scripture. Although these Scriptures may have other applications, we sensed the Holy Spirit was using them to teach us about new church structures.

> *No one puts a piece of unshrunk cloth on an old garment; for the patch pulls away from the garment, and the tear is made worse. Nor do they put new wine into old wineskins, or else the wineskins break, the wine is spilled, and the wine-skins are ruined. But they put new wine into new wine-skins, and both are preserved (Matthew 9:16-17).*

This "new wineskin" we believed, was to be a new model of church structure, tailor-made to serve the new believers in Jesus Christ. And what better place to meet than in a home!

A wineskin is like a balloon. It needs to be flexible and pliable. Putting a new Christian (new wine) into an old struc-ture can cause the structure to break and the new Christian may be lost. New Christians should be placed in new struc-tures that are flexible and able to encourage their spiritual growth.

Are You Willing to Be Involved in the Underground Church?

One day in 1978, I took a break from farm work and youth ministry duties in order to pray for a few hours. I was startled when I heard the Lord speak to me through His still, small voice. "Are you willing to be involved in the underground church?" He asked. I was shocked. The words that I heard in my spirit were distinct, even piercing!

When the Lord spoke to me, although the words were clear, I didn't understand what He was trying to tell me. My mind raced immediately to the Berlin Wall, and the barbed wire fences that then surrounded the borders of many communist nations. I thought of the persecuted church meeting under-ground in nations that opposed the gospel. It still didn't make sense, yet I knew I had to respond: I had heard the call of God.

"Yes, Lord," I replied as tears formed in my eyes. "I am willing." I chose to obey, even though I didn't understand what it all meant.

Soon after the Lord spoke to me about the underground church, I asked some of my Christian friends if they would be willing to meet with me each week for the purpose of enhancing our own spiritual growth. Two men responded. We began meeting every week for prayer, Bible study, encouragement and mutual accountability. Within the next few years this "house fellowship" grew, and we started to reach out to new believers. Soon our living room was filled to capacity.

With leadership established in the first group, eventually, my wife LaVerne and I were "commissioned out" to help another couple start a second small group. These groups served as a place for new believers to be nurtured and taught the Word of God. We had no desire to start another church. We felt there were enough churches in our community.

Then one Sunday morning in January of 1980, while sitting in our local Mennonite church near Lititz, Pennsylvania, the Lord spoke to me through His still, small voice. As I was waiting for the service to begin, the Lord spoke these words clearly to my spirit, "It's time to start something new."

Although I had grown up in the Church of the Brethren, this was the congregation that I had become a part of when we were married. I had married the pastor's daughter, served a year in the denomination's mission program on an island off the coast of South Carolina during our first year of marriage, and was a song leader for the Sunday services. Although much of our time was taken up during the week reaching out to young people through a local para-church youth ministry, we had a genuine love and appreciation for God's people at our church.

Nevertheless, I took this word from the Lord very seriously. After the service was over, a friend unexpectedly invited me to a meeting of church leaders the following day. At that meeting, I had the opportunity to meet the president of a local mission board who desired to see new churches planted. His encouragement spurred me on.

I told the other leaders of the two house fellowships that I sensed the Lord had called me to start something new. Others who were involved in youth ministry with us and still others in the body of Christ in our area who had a similar vision came together to pray each week. It seemed clear that there was a need for a New Testament church that could be structured so it could be flexible enough to relate to believers from all backgrounds and assist them in their spiritual growth.

In the process of time, I slowly began to understand what the Lord had in mind when He asked me if I was willing to be involved in the underground church. An underground church is like a tree: its trunk, branches and leaves are only half of the picture. The unnoticed half, the underground root system, nourishes the whole tree and keeps it healthy.

The underground church, we began to realize, was to consist of believers gathered together through a structure of small cell groups meeting in homes to pray, evangelize and build relationships with one another. In this way, each believer is made an active and vital part of the body of Christ.

When every believer is nourished and healthy, the whole church is strong. As water and nutrients feed the tree by climbing up through the root system, so the church is nourished and strengthened by what happens in the underground, or the unseen realm of church life—believers involved in cell groups in homes. It was becoming clear that these relationships in cell groups would not be an appendage of the church, but in actuality, they would be the basic building blocks of the church. Everything else was secondary.

When Jesus cursed the fig tree, nothing appeared to happen immediately; however, the following day the tree was withered and dead. Probably the roots underground had dried up and died instantly, but it took until the next day for the leaves to wither and die due to the lack of water that came up through the root system.

The enemy seeks to destroy the church in the same way—from underground. He attempts to use broken relationships and to attack the lives of individual believers in order to weaken God's people. But when the part of the church that is underground is strong, then the whole church will be strong and continue to grow.

Time to Step Out in Faith

In October of 1980, our group of approximately twenty-five believers met for the first time for a Sunday morning celebration in a living room. Five families had been commissioned out of our local Mennonite church the week before to start this "new church." A small band of others also joined us at the inception of the new work.

We didn't have a name for our group until a woman in our cell group was praying and received a vision from the Lord. In this vision, she clearly saw four distinct capital letters with a period behind each letter [D.O.V.E.]. It appeared that the Lord was giving our new church a name.

Personally, I struggled with the name "DOVE." A church with a bird's name was not exactly appealing to me! We continued to pray, and after much deliberation it became clear, whether I liked it or not, God had spoken and we needed to obey. We sensed that DOVE was an acronym meaning "Declaring Our Victory Emmanuel."

"DOVE Fellowship" had officially begun. There was an aura of excitement among us as we met in three separate home groups during the week, pursuing the vision that the Lord had given. But there were also times of pain. Within the first year, the three original house groups became two. Instead of the groups growing and multiplying, it seemed like we were going backwards. We soon realized that we had a lack of clear leadership for the group, causing confusion.

False Humility

We had encouraged the believers in the first house fellowships to designate no one person as a leader, but instead to choose a team that would provide coequal leadership. Each cell had two coequal leaders, and the church at large was led by six coequal leaders. On the surface, this sounded good and noble; in reality, it was a manifestation of false humility. Underneath the surface, there was struggle.

It's funny to recall now, but with six of us leading, we discovered on one Sunday morning that we couldn't come to a decision about who should preach the Word in our celebration meeting. Since none of us were giving clear leadership, no one preached! It would be fine for no one to preach if the Lord was truly leading in this way; however, when it is by default, it causes confusion and stress among the body of Christ. This type of leadership structure will either cause a move of God to stop, or it will slow it down until there is clarity regarding God-ordained leadership.

Harold Eberle, in *The Complete Wineskin*, says it like this:

> *After observing many, many churches, I can personally tell you that no matter what form of government a church claims to have, there is always one person who openly or quietly holds the greatest influence over the church. Setting up the proper government is never a matter of keeping it out of the hands of one person, but putting it into the hands of God's person.* [1]

Within the first year, this "leaderless group" came to the difficult realization that there was a need for clear, delegated leadership among us. Although we continued to believe that team leadership was important, we recognized the need for "headship" on each leadership team. Two spiritual leaders from our locality who had agreed to oversee and serve our fledgling group helped us through these difficult times. Two from the group of the original six co-leaders were set apart as leaders of the church and were ordained by a local denomination which was committed to supporting us during these early years. I was acknowledged as the primary leader of the leadership team.

During the next ten years after its bumpy start, this local church became known in our community as DOVE Christian Fellowship, and by the grace of God grew to well over 2000 believers scattered throughout communities in a seven-county area of Pennsylvania. These believers met in more than 100 cell groups during the week and on Sunday mornings met in clusters of cells (congregations) in five different locations. The whole church came together five or six times each year on a Sunday morning in a large gymnasium or at a local park amphitheater for a corporate celebration. There was a real sense of excitement and enthusiasm about the things of God.

Whenever clusters of cells (congregations) renting facilities for Sunday morning "celebrations" outgrew a building, we either moved to a larger one or started two or three celebration meetings in the same building on a Sunday. But the focus was not on the Sunday morning meetings. The focus was on the church meeting from house to house throughout our communities each week.

Our goal was to multiply the cells and celebrations and begin new Sunday morning celebrations and new cell groups in other areas as God gave the increase. We also found that by renting buildings at an economical dollar figure, we had more money available to use for world missions. During these years, churches were planted in Scotland, Brazil, and Kenya. These overseas churches were built on Jesus Christ and on these same underground house-to-house principles.

Learning the Hard Way

Then the storms began to mount. There seemed to be an undercurrent that constantly sapped me and others in leadership of strength and vision. It was subtle—happening without us even realizing what was taking place—and it was hard to put our fingers on it. I found myself increasingly making decisions that were based more on the desires of others than on what I really believed was the Lord's direction for us as a church.

People began to leave, not in vast numbers, but one family at a time. Even some of those who served in areas of leadership were leaving to find new direction in their lives. More and more, I felt pressed into a mold.

Jim Petersen, in *Church Without Walls*, clearly describes some of what happened to us during these difficult years. Although he was talking about another fellowship, his story closely paralleled ours.

> *I have a friend who was a part of a team that set out to start a church . . . The congregation was divided into house churches, each of which was assigned an elder who helped shepherd the members of that house church. Centralized activities were kept at a minimum for the sake of keeping people free to minister to their families and unbelieving friends.*

The weekly meetings were dynamic. I will never forget the first one I visited. People of all sorts were there, from men in business suits to ponytails. Many were new believers. The Bible teaching was down to earth, aimed at people's needs. I loved it.

So did most everyone else who visited. The word got around and soon the migratory flock from neighboring churches came pouring in. Their needs consumed the energies of the leaders of this young church. Their wants gradually set the agenda. The inertia of the traditions of these migrants engulfed this very creative effort and shaped it accordingly . . . So what's the problem, we ask? The problem is that the vision that original team had for taking the church into society through the efforts of every believer was frustrated. [2]

Like this church, our vision, too, was frustrated. From the beginning, we had felt instructed of the Lord to reach the lost and disciple new Christians. Developing new wineskins for new wine was a priority. But we found ourselves becoming more and more distracted by the many voices around us.

Another trap we fell into was adopting methods we had seen work in other churches when the Lord had not called us to do the same thing. It has been said that "we can never attempt to implement another man's program, unless we first learn to adopt his values." This is true. We learned the hard way that it is of utmost importance to adopt Christ's value system, and hear from Him and Him alone, for the direction we should take as a church.

During the spring of 1991, we took time to pray and re-evaluate. For more than a year we went into a maintenance mode as a church. As we continued to seek God's face, we began to come to grips with what the Lord was trying to tell us.

Getting Back on Track

A major breakthrough came when my wife, LaVerne, and I retreated to the mountains to pray during the early part of 1992. The Lord clearly revealed to LaVerne that we had not properly fulfilled the charge He had given us 12 years before.

He had called us at that time to build the "underground church" by focusing on the formation of new "wineskins" for the new believers that were being brought into the kingdom of God. We had become sidetracked from this original vision. We cried out to the Lord for forgiveness and received His cleansing. A few months later, I had an encounter with the Lord that I describe in Chapter 15 of this book.

Despite our many mistakes, the Lord has remained ever faithful. By His grace, we are getting back on track, working to fulfill His call to build the "underground church." As a leadership team and as a church, the Lord has given us the grace to again walk together in unity to fulfill His purposes. We are grateful to the Lord for giving us another chance.

The Lord provided a fresh vision to reach out to the nations as we labored to fulfill the Great Commission. In November 1992, DOVE Christian Fellowship New Zealand (DCF New Zealand) was birthed through believers meeting in cell groups from house to house.

In 1995, at the first printing of this book, DOVE Christian Fellowship in Pennsylvania was made up of believers who met in eight "congregations" (clusters of cells) throughout south-central Pennsylvania with cell churches planted in Scotland, Brazil, Kenya and New Zealand. Today, the church is a network of cell-based churches worldwide. Each congregation and each cell group has its own personality as they focus on knowing the Lord Jesus and on fulfilling the Great Commission. Flexibility is encouraged.

Although we transitioned into a family of cell-based churches in 1996 (see Chapter 16 update), cell groups continue to provide our basic structure as we seek to reach out beyond ourselves to win the lost and to make disciples for Jesus Christ. Intercession is a priority as we realize that the struggles that God's people face are not with flesh and blood, but with principalities and powers in heavenly places. As cell groups are constantly growing and multiplying, leadership training is also a very important part of our mission.

Learning From Our Mistakes

Over the years, we have learned many times from our experiences and mistakes. In some ways, it feels like the longer we go, the less we know. And yet, the Lord is faithful to teach us. We are constantly learning. *House to House* candidly describes both our victories and our mistakes. Hopefully, it will keep you from making some of the same blunders.

God continues to teach us how He can build His kingdom through us as a cell-based church. We want to share with others what God is showing us because He is a creative God and constantly gives new insights to His people. We want to emphasize that we do not believe we have "cornered the market" on how God will move in these last days. We are well aware that God is using many types of churches and ministries to advance His kingdom into the 21st century. Our prayer is that we all work together, listening to and depending on the Holy Spirit to direct our steps.

Use This Book as a Guide for Cell Ministry

Much of what you read throughout *House to House* may serve as a type of handbook to which you can refer in the days ahead. If you are a cell group leader, an assistant cell leader, or a potential cell leader, you will find that this book does not have all the answers. It is simply a guide to use as you rely on the Holy Spirit to lead you in the building of the Church of Jesus Christ. If you sense that the Lord may be calling you to labor with Him to build His church from house-to-house according to this underground pattern, my desire is that the Lord will use these scriptural principles and practical suggestions to spur you on.

In the next chapter, we will begin by looking at the challenge you and I face in coming to understand God's priorities for our Christian lives.

Questions to think about
from Chapter One

1. Describe a wineskin.

2. Using the tree as a picture of the present day underground church, how does the process of spiritual nourishment operate?

3. Are you being nourished spiritually? Explain.

4. Are you nourishing others? How?

5. What is the importance of a church having a vision?

6. What is the most important or most appealing aspect of the underground church to you?

CHAPTER 2

GOD'S PRIORITIES

Then the eleven disciples went away into Galilee, to the mountain which Jesus had appointed for them. When they saw Him, they worshipped Him; but some doubted. And Jesus came and spoke to them, saying, "All authority has been given to Me in heaven and on earth. Go therefore and make disciples of all the nations, baptizing them in the name of the Father and of the Son and of the Holy Spirit, teaching them to observe all things that I have commanded you; and lo, I am with you always, even to the end of the age." Amen (Matthew 28:16-20).

Our natural tendency is to look for formulas and methods to fulfill the Lord's plans. However, the more we grow in the Lord, the more we realize that our way of thinking with our natural minds is often not at all what the Lord has in mind. So before we get into some of the basic principles that we have learned about cell group leadership, let's begin with God's priorities.

Ecclesiastes 4:12 tells us, "a threefold cord is not quickly broken." The three strands that we believe form the core of the Christian life are *prayer* (knowing God), *evangelism* (reaching the lost), and *discipleship* (training new believers).

Prayer—Knowing God

God has called us to know Him, first and foremost! Matthew 28 tells us that Jesus appointed a certain place to meet with His disciples. And when they saw Him, they worshipped Him. Jesus has called us to meet with Him and worship Him each day. The Lord tells us in John 17:3 that eternal life is to know Him. Our number one priority must be to know Him personally through time spent with Him each day, or cell group ministry will become just another church program.

Dr. Yonggi Cho is the pastor of the world's largest church in Seoul, Korea. Dr. Cho has spoken to thousands of pastors and church leaders in America during the past few years. I have heard him say that American pastors are attentive when he speaks on cell group principles, but when he begins to teach on prayer and communion with the Holy Spirit, the pastors put their pencils down and stop taking notes. They lose interest. The spiritual principles and guidelines outlined in this book will only be effective as long as we are in love with Jesus and communing with Him every day.

Often when I speak at churches and conferences, I am not able to take LaVerne with me. I find great joy in searching through my luggage for a special love note that she often has hidden in my bags. I love reading those notes, because I'm in love with her. If I no longer desired to read those love notes, it would be a warning light that my love for her is waning. Do you love to read your love letters from Jesus? That is what the Bible is all about. It is filled with love letters from the God who loves us.

Jesus says in Matthew 4:4, "Man shall not live by bread alone, but by every word that proceeds from the mouth of God." I need a fresh word from the Lord every day. If I am living on last week's manna, I will begin to get weak and even sick spiritually. Only healthy Christians will have something to give to others. And there is no substitute. We must cultivate our relationship with our Lord Jesus every day.

Evangelism—Reaching the Lost

Jesus spent much of His time with the tax collectors and the sinners of His day. His heart went out to those who were lost. The people who hated Jesus were not the sinners, but the scribes and the Pharisees, the religious leaders. Many times, the church today seems to focus more on church politics, personal opinions, and self-preservation than on the priorities of Jesus.

The Bible says, " . . . For this purpose the Son of God was manifested, that He might destroy the works of the devil" (I John 3:8). The works of the devil are everywhere. Our communities are filled with broken lives, fear, abuse, broken relationships, perversion, the murdering of unborn children, materialism and lust. Jesus came for the purpose of destroying these works!

We must understand that our heart motivation for being involved in cell group ministry must be the same as that of our Lord Jesus—to destroy the works of the devil. Jesus is the answer to every problem. He is the great Redeemer. He came to restore completely every man, woman and child who will open up their hearts and lives to Him. The Scriptures tell us, "How shall they believe in Him of whom they have not heard?" We are commissioned by our Lord Jesus Christ to reach the lost of our generation. Cell group ministry is one of the spiritual tools to assist us in fulfilling this mandate from the Lord.

Jesus told His disciples in Matthew 28 to "Go," knowing that all authority had been given to Him in heaven and on earth. He promised to be with them always, just as He will always be with us. Often Christians do not sense the Lord's presence with them. Could it be they are so caught up in the cares of this world that they feel unable to obey the commandment to go and share the good news of Jesus with those who are lost?

Lord, we need a revival. We need to get our priorities in line with Your priorities.

Discipleship—Training New Believers

Jesus commands us in Matthew 28:19 to ". . . make disciples of all the nations, baptizing them in the name of the Father and of the Son and of the Holy Spirit, teaching them to observe all things that I have commanded you." Unless we have a clear understanding that making disciples is near the top of God's priority list, cell group ministry will be just another religious program.

Jesus had a vision to revolutionize the world—person to person, house to house. Out of the multitudes of His followers, He appointed only twelve to be His disciples.

Then He appointed twelve, that they might be with Him and that He might send them out to preach (Mark 3:14).

By living closely with them, day in and day out, He gave them intense training, demonstrated His miraculous power, explained His parables, and answered their questions.

A disciple is a learner, an apprentice. Jesus provided His disciples with innumerable opportunities to practice and exercise the things He taught them. He poured His life into them by close, daily contact for three years. As we observe Jesus interacting with these twelve men, we see a model of what could be regarded as the first cell group in the history of the church!

The Lord commands us to go and do likewise. Whatever He has taught us, we are to teach to others. This not only applies to Bible knowledge, but to practical Christianity. The most effective way for you to teach a young husband how to love and honor his wife is for you to love and honor *your* wife. The best way for you to teach another Christian how to have a clear financial budget is for you to show him how *you* set up a budget. If you believe the Lord has called you to teach a new Christian to pray, pray with him! We teach others by modeling biblical truths with our own lives.

The Bible gives many examples of discipleship. Paul, the apostle, took young Timothy with him as a disciple (Acts 16). Later, Timothy was sent out to do the same: take the truths that he learned from Paul and impart them to others (II Timothy 2:2). Moses had Joshua as his disciple for forty years, preparing Joshua for leadership. Elijah found Elisha and became his mentor. The list goes on and on. The Lord is restoring the truth of loving discipleship to His church today. He has called us to make disciples.

Christianity is not just sitting in a pew each Sunday morning, looking at the back of someone's head. Christianity is knowing Jesus, reaching out to the lost and making disciples. This must be the motivation of our hearts in order to fulfill effectively the Lord's purposes for us as believers in Jesus Christ. You will discover the three strands of prayer, evangelism and discipleship woven throughout these pages; they will surface again and again.

"I'm ready!" you say. "I understand the challenge to make disciples, and believe that small groups are an effective way to build the church. But exactly what does the Bible tell us about small groups? What is the biblical plan of training through small groups?" Read on!

Questions to think about
from Chapter Two

1. What place does prayer have in your daily life?

2. Describe how prayer, evangelism and discipleship help fulfill the Great Commission.

3. In what ways are you moved to do something about the needs in your community? Be specific.

4. When have you recently shared with another what Jesus means to you?

5. What does being a disciple mean to you?

6. In what ways are you discipling others?

Our Vision

To build a relationship

with Jesus,

with one another,

and to reach the world from

house to house,

city to city,

nation to nation.

CHAPTER 3

A BIBLICAL VISION
FOR CELL GROUPS

To be most effective in building His church, we believe that it is God's plan for us to follow Jesus' model of training through small groups. Just as a cell is one of the smallest units in the physical body, so we have chosen to use the term "cell groups" to denote the small units of the local church where relationships and personal growth take place.

Cell groups give everyone an opportunity to get involved. In cell groups, each person has the opportunity to begin to fulfill the purpose God has for his life. The cell group is the place where he can receive training, instruction and encouragement as he reaches out to his friends and neighbors with the Good News of Jesus Christ.

We have used the cell group model to build God's kingdom from the inception of our church. Although we initially used the term, "house fellowships," we were following the same spiritual principles. Cell groups are not simply a program of the church; they are a place where people have the chance to experience and demonstrate New Testament Christianity built on relationships, not simply on meetings. In cell groups, people share their lives together and reach out with the healing love of Jesus to a broken world. Our vision as a church is to **build a relationship with Jesus, with one another, and to reach the world from house to house, city to city, nation to nation.** Since the principles of God's Word are applicable and adaptable to any culture, nation or people group, we believe the following guidelines and principles will be helpful to you no matter where you live as you reach the world for Jesus from house to house.

The House to House Principle

In Acts 2:41, the Scriptures tell us:

> *Then those who gladly received his word were baptized; and that day about three thousand souls were added to them.*

How could the 120 disciples in the upper room possibly have taken care of 3,000 new believers? Part of their secret is found in Acts 2:46-47:

> *So continuing daily with one accord in the temple, and breaking bread from **house to house,** they ate their food with gladness and simplicity of heart, praising God and having favor with all the people. And the Lord added to the church daily those who were being saved.*

God's people gathered at the temple and met in small groups in homes, "and they continued steadfastly in the apostles' doctrine and fellowship, in the breaking of bread, and in prayers" (Acts 2:42). They began to minister to one another and to the unsaved on an individual basis, and the Lord kept adding to the church daily! In Acts 20:20, the Apostle Paul declares to members of the church at Ephesus that, "I kept back nothing that was helpful, but proclaimed it to you, and taught you publicly and from house to house."

The letter that Paul wrote to the Christians in Rome was written to believers in Jesus Christ who met in peoples' homes. In his letter to the Romans, Paul indicates that one of these groups met in the home of Priscilla and Aquila:

> *Greet Priscilla and Aquila, my fellow workers in Christ Jesus, who risked their own necks for my life, to whom not only I give thanks, but also all the churches of the Gentiles. Likewise greet **the church that is in their house.** (Romans 16:3-5).*

Paul also sent his greetings to the household of Aristobulus and the household of Narcissus (Romans 16:10-11). When Paul wrote to his friend Philemon, he expressed his greetings to the church in his house, " . . . to the beloved Apphia, Archippus our fellow soldier, and to the church in your house" (Philemon 1:2).

Periodically, down through the ages, the church has lost the New Testament component of meeting in small groups in the homes of individual believers and has placed an emphasis on the church as it meets in large buildings. In his book *The Open Church*, James H. Rutz says:

> It was in 323 AD, almost three hundred years after the birth of the church, that Christians first met in something we now call a "church building." For all three hundred years before that, the church met in living rooms!
>
> Constantine built these assembly buildings for Christians not only in Constantinople, but also in Rome, Jerusalem, and in many parts of Italy, all between 323 and 327! This then triggered a massive "church building" fad in large cities all over the Empire. [3]

Temple ministry is beneficial for corporate worship, teaching and celebration, but we believe that the Lord wants us to get back to seeing the church as people, not as a place where believers meet. Our homes, places of business, schools, and other circles of contact provide excellent places for the church to meet as we infiltrate our spheres of influence with the gospel of Jesus Christ.

What Was The Early Church Really Like?

T.L. Osborne, in his book, *Soul-winning, Out Where the Sinners Are* tells the story of a possible conversation with Aquila in Ephesus, from the book of Acts:

> "Good evening, Aquila. We understand you're a member of the church here. Could we come in and visit for a while?"
>
> "Certainly. Come in."
>
> "If you don't mind, we would like for you to tell us about the way the churches here in Asia Minor carry on their soul-winning program. We read that you have been a member of a church in Corinth and Rome, as well as this one here in Ephesus. You should be very qualified to tell us about evangelism in the New Testament Church. If you don't mind, we'd like to visit your church while we're here."
>
> "Sit down, you're already in the church. It meets in my home."

"You don't have a church building?"

"What's a church building? No, I guess we don't."

"Tell me Aquila, what is your church doing to evangelize Ephesus? What are you doing to reach the city with the gospel?"

"Oh, we already evangelized Ephesus. Every person in the city clearly understands the Gospel . . . We just visited every home in the city. That's the way the church in Jerusalem first evangelized that city (Acts 5:42). The disciples there evangelized the entire city of Jerusalem in a very short time. All the other churches in Asia Minor have followed that example." [4]

The church of today should take a lesson from the early church. Today's church has tried to reach people for Christ in our communities with extravagant church programs and 20th century methodology. While such methods have their place, they can never substitute for personal relationships formed in the context of genuine Christian community.

Recently, a couple who are cell leaders in our church began a ministry in the heart of a city in our local area. A man who has lived in this city all his life shared an observation that illustrates our point. He noted that many of the city churches have moved to the suburbs while others have sought to promote programs encouraging city dwellers to "come in." He was grateful to see that the heart of this couple and their work is to move in among the community and develop relationships in order to share the gospel.

Don't you think it's time to get back to basics and allow God to build His church through New Testament discipling relationships? It's not too late.

Living Stones

Coming to Him as to a living stone, rejected indeed by men, but chosen by God and precious, you also, as living stones, are being built up a spiritual house, a holy priesthood, to offer up spiritual sacrifices acceptable to God through Jesus Christ (I Peter 2:4-5).

The Bible calls us "living stones." Each believer has been made alive through faith in our Lord Jesus Christ. The Lord builds us together with other Christians into a type of spiritual house or community. Christianity is practical. Who are the other living stones the Lord has built you with?

Do you know that as "living stones" we can demobilize the devil as we obey the living God? Imagine a large stone wall made up of thousands of stones mortared together. These thousands of stones are made up of clusters of stones that touch one another. Can you imagine how frightening it would be if each of these stones were alive and all decided to walk toward you at the same time? That is how the devil feels when, as Christians, we pull together, realize God has called us to minister to one another and obey the prompting of the Holy Spirit to destroy the works of darkness.

Each (living) stone can only touch a small group of other believers at one time. These believers are knit together in small groups through relationships as they are united in the Lord. Ten people who are of one mind and heart can have a tremendous impact on the kingdom of darkness. The devil would like to get us alone, to isolate us, leaving us without the support of our brothers and sisters in Christ.

In small groups, we can interact meaningfully with a few other people (saved and unsaved) through encouragement, prayer and practical service. As each cell group obeys our Lord Jesus, the entire church will have a powerful effect on our communities as we minister in Jesus' name. It's important to remember that the "ministers" Paul speaks about in the New Testament are not only the pastors or leaders—they include all the saints!

> *And He Himself gave some to be apostles, some prophets, some evangelists, and some pastors and teachers, for the equipping of the saints for the work of ministry, for the edifying of the body of Christ (Ephesians 4:11-12).*

God has called every believer to be a minister. He calls apostles, prophets, evangelists, pastors and teachers to teach and train others how to minister. You and I, average, down-to-earth believers in Jesus, are called of the Lord to minister to people. This ministry becomes effective in a small group setting as we will see in Chapter 8.

Learning From History—The Methodist Revival

I have had the privilege of proclaiming the gospel on six continents during the past few years. Amazingly, in every nation that I go, I find a Methodist Church building! Some of my Methodist friends tell me that many of these buildings serve as memorials to a past revival. What happened?

Howard A. Snyder, in *The Radical Wesley* says it like this:

> John Wesley [the founder of the Methodist Church], saw that new wine must be put into new wineskins. So the story of Wesley's life and ministry is the story of creating and adapting structures to serve the burgeoning revival movement.
>
> After thirty years, in 1768, Methodism had 40 circuits and 27,341 members . . . By 1798, seven years after Wesley's death, the totals had jumped to 149 circuits with 101,712 members. By the turn of the century, about one in every thirty Englishmen were Methodists.

A key to the Methodist revival was the accountability that each of these new believers found in small groups. Wesley called them class meetings.

> The classes were in effect house churches . . . meeting in various neighborhoods where people lived. The class leaders (men and women) were disciplers.
>
> The classes normally met one evening each week for an hour or so. Each person reported on his or her spiritual progress, or on particular needs or problems, and received the support and prayers of the others . . . According to one author it was, in fact, in the class meeting "where the great majority of conversions occurred."
>
> The class meeting system tied together the widely scattered Methodist people and became the sustainer of the Methodist renewal over many decades. The movement was in fact a whole series of sporadic and often geographically localized revivals which were interconnected and spread by the society and class network, rather than one continuous wave of revival which swept the country. [Classes joined together to form a society.]

Without the class meeting, the scattered fires of revival would have burned out long before the movement was able to make a deep impact on the nation . . .

Now here is the remarkable thing. One hears today that it is hard to find enough leaders for small groups or for those to carry on the other responsibilities in the church. Wesley put one in ten, perhaps one in five, to work in significant ministry and leadership. And who were these people? Not the educated or the wealthy with time on their hands, but laboring men and women, husbands and wives and young folks with little or no training, but with spiritual gifts and eagerness to serve . . .

The system which emerged gave lie to the argument that you can't build a church on poor and uneducated folk. Not only did Wesley reach the masses; he made leaders of thousands of them. [5]

Slowly the Methodist believers began to put more of an emphasis on the Sunday morning church meetings in their buildings. As they de-emphasized the accountable relationships they had in their class meetings, the revival movement began to decline. God, help us to not make the same mistake in this generation! Let us learn from history that small groups have often served to fan revival throughout church history:

The ember that has rekindled movements of renewal ever since [the first century] is the cell group or "microcommunity," as church historian Richard Lovelace calls the small group of believers that meets for prayer and support. As we seek to ignite a discipling movement in our own time, we must place the local prayer and support group concept at the very center of our strategy. The great reformer Martin Luther proposed that widespread spiritual renewal should take the form of ecclesiolae in ecclesia—little churches within the church. [6]

Tradition, Tradition!

Tevye, the patriarch in the classic motion picture, *The Fiddler on the Roof*, loved tradition. If something has worked in the past, most people, like Tevye, are happy to continue on in the same way. The old adage, "If it isn't broken, it doesn't need to be fixed," satisfies many Christians today as they continue on in old patterns of church structure.

As an "underground church," DOVE Christian Fellowship is set up in a nontraditional structure of home cell groups. In our desire to pattern ourselves after the New Testament church, we have deviated from traditional church structure. Yet, in one way we have conceded to the tradition around us, namely that of meeting every Sunday morning for a celebration in local congregations (clusters of cells).

Would you dare to dream for a minute about other options? Yes, tradition tells us that believers should meet in a church building on Sunday mornings, but according to the Scriptures the believers in the New Testament appear to have met in homes on Sunday mornings. Church history tells us that the believers met on the first day of the week. But since the emphasis seemed to be on the house to house ministry, and they didn't have their own buildings until about 250 years later, it seems reasonable to believe that the believers met in homes on Sundays.

We are not implying that it is wrong for congregations to meet in a building on a Sunday morning. Our culture is accustomed to Christians gathering in a church building every Sunday—there's nothing wrong about it. A concern we should have is this: Do we meet together in this way because the Holy Spirit has moved us to or because tradition has dictated it?

Certainly, not all tradition is wrong: Some traditions are godly and good. When traditions take on a life of their own, however, we may be in trouble, because we begin to trust a method rather than the Living God. Even cell groups can become legalistic and traditional if we trust the method rather than allow God to keep us flexible and open to His leading.

I look forward to the day when we can be so flexible that we will allow a church building to be utilized every day of the week. One congregation (cluster of cell groups) could use the building on a Sunday morning. Another group could use it on Sunday night. Six other groups could use it the other six nights of the week. A group could even use it on Saturday morning. Imagine the same building being used by nine different congregations! That's divine efficiency!

The believers could meet in cell groups in homes on Sunday mornings. All of the money that is saved on renting and maintaining buildings could be given to missions and to the poor! Or the truly radical could use Sunday morning to sleep in or play golf with an unsaved neighbor. Believers could meet together on a Sunday evening as a cell group and then meet as a congregation during a night of the week. Of course, if houses are large enough, some congregations could have their regular meetings in homes. That would release all kinds of money for missions!

Ralph Neighbour, in *The Seven Last Words of the Church*, makes some important observations about the church's dependence on buildings:

> *Churches in the United States now own in excess of $102 billion in land and buildings. I am not picking on my denomination, but simply using it as an example: We will spend far more than $50 million this year simply to pay the interest on church mortgages. This profit by bankers from churches represents an investment which is several million dollars more than the amount to be invested by those churches for all home and foreign mission causes.* [7]

Recently our leadership team did a study from the Bible on the use of the tithe. To our amazement, we could not find even one reference in the entire Bible that encouraged using tithe money for buildings. The references that were given showed us that tithe money was to be used for supporting people, and then offerings were to be taken for buildings. Although most of the money that our church has spent during these past years on buildings has been on rent instead of on mortgages, we realized recently that we were spending too much of the tithes on buildings. Without becoming dogmatic regarding this principle, we must take a close look at how we are spending the Lord's money so that we can see the church built from house to house.

The Jethro Principle

Moses was wearing himself out by continually listening to and solving the disputes and dilemmas which arose among the Israelites. He was weighed down by the responsibilities that came with serving more than three million people. The Israelites were burdened by having to wait day after day for Moses to hear their case. This reminds me of many pastors today. Many church leaders are nearing burnout, as they try all by themselves to juggle the crushing ministry responsibilities of the church.

God gave Moses, through Jethro, wisdom to rule so that he and the people would not be worn out. Jethro suggested a simple solution: Able men were to be selected from among the people to listen to any problems which arose, solve the ones they could handle, and pass on the most difficult cases to Moses.

> *Moreover you shall select from all the people able men, such as fear God, men of truth, hating covetousness; and place such over them to be rulers of thousands, rulers of hundreds, rulers of fifties, and rulers of tens. And let them judge the people at all times. Then it will be that every great matter they shall bring to you, but every small matter they themselves shall judge. So it will be easier for you, for they will bear the burden with you. If you do this thing, and God so commands you, then you will be able to endure, and all this people will also go to their place in peace. So Moses heeded the voice of his father-in-law and did all that he had said (Exodus 18:21-24).*

There would be one judge for each 1000 people. Moses would appoint ten additional judges under him, each in charge of a hundred; and under each of them would be two judges, each responsible for the affairs of fifty people. Each of these would have five judges beneath him, each counseling ten persons. Only the most severe or perplexing problems got all the way up to Moses, who alone had the God-given abilities to handle them.

We do not believe that it is necessary to set up a legalistic system in the church that looks exactly like the structure that Moses used; however, we are convinced that we need to see the church from God's perspective and use the wisdom He has given us in determining its structure. Our God set the sun and the moon and the stars in place: He is a God of order.

The early apostles understood the principle of delegation that Moses had used many years before. During the great revival that took place in the book of Acts, the apostles soon found it necessary to delegate authority and responsibility to others so that they could concentrate on their top priority—prayer and the ministry of the Word.

> *Then the twelve summoned the multitude of the disciples and said, "It is not desirable that we should leave the word of God and serve tables. Therefore, brethren, seek out from among you seven men of good reputation, full of the Holy Spirit and wisdom, whom we may appoint over this business; but we will give ourselves continually to prayer and to the ministry of the word" (Acts 6:2-4).*

Many times today, those in primary leadership in the church are so caught up in management that they do not have time to pray and give clear direction to the work of God. Applying the Jethro principle to the local church today would result in the delegation of authority and responsibility to believers on the "front-lines" of ministry, who are best prepared to make such decisions anyway. Unless pastors can release responsibility and authority to the servant-leaders at a small group level, this principle will not work. Although local elders or pastors are responsible before the Lord for God's people in the cells, the cell leaders must be released and trusted with the care of the people of God within their cell.

When Dr. Cho from Seoul, Korea, was at our church in south-central Pennsylvania for a pastors' conference, I talked to him about the need to release local leadership in a small group setting. I will never forget his response. "Many pastors are threatened," he said. "They are afraid to release their people."

Moses gave Pharaoh the mandate of the Lord: "Let my people go!" I believe that the Lord is setting every believer free to be an able minister of the new covenant. May every spiritual leader maintain his security in the Lord and take the risk to release the people of God to minister to others.

Once servant-leaders release people to minister, the church will grow by leaps and bounds, as it did at the first. But be prepared: with growth comes growing pains; with risk comes both success and failure. Even in the midst of inevitable set-backs, however, be encouraged, for failure is part of the process.

As the church grows, it is important for each believer to know where he fits in the body of Christ. In the next chapter, we will discuss how God places us within spiritual families.

Note: In order to facilitate easier reading of this book, I will generally use the masculine gender when referring to leaders in the church. For the record, we firmly believe that women today are given a spiritual mandate to lead just as many women in the early church labored as leaders.

Questions to think about
from Chapter Three

1. Use your imagination: What was a first century church meeting like?

2. Compare the church made of living stones with a church building made of brick or stone.

3. What are some practical and financial reasons for limiting the number of big church buildings?

4. Explain the "Jethro principle."

5. What did Dr. Cho mean when he said that some pastors are afraid to release their people?

CHAPTER 4

SPIRITUAL FAMILIES

After crossing the Jordan, Joshua and the Israelites captured Jericho, and then proceeded towards Ai, where they experienced a humiliating defeat. Joshua cried out to God, and the Lord told him that there was sin in the camp. It is important to notice how the Lord instructed Joshua to identify the man who was in sin. The Lord could have simply pointed him out to Joshua, but He didn't. Instead, Joshua had to go through tribes, clans, and families until he arrived at the guilty individual. There are levels of accountability in the kingdom of God.

> *So Joshua rose early in the morning and brought Israel by their tribes, and the tribe of Judah was taken. He brought the clan of Judah, and he took the family of the Zarhites; and he brought the family of the Zarhites man by man, and Zabdi was taken. Then he brought his household man by man, and Achan the son of Carmi, the son of Zabdi, the son of Zerah, of the tribe of Judah, was taken (Joshua 7:16-18).*

The Lord sees His people much differently than we often perceive them. The Lord sees us, first of all, as individual believers, bought by the blood of Jesus. But He also sees His people within spiritual families. All families have extended families. My immediate family lives with me in the same house. We spend a lot of time together. On occasion we spend time with our parents and brothers and sisters and their children. Once each year we spend time with some of our cousins and their children. I don't even know all of these people by name, but they are still a part of my family! By only meeting in congregations on Sunday mornings, the church of today is emphasizing the extended spiritual family rather than the immediate spiritual family (small groups with people we know well).

The question we need to ask is this: How can these spiritual families be most effective? Part of the answer to this question is to be found in recognizing that the Lord sees each of us as a part of various spiritual spheres.

First of all, He sees us as members of a natural family. In God's plan, families (spouses and children) are to function as little churches. Nearly everything the church does our family should do. In my own family, we teach, pray and share our faith with the unsaved. Sometimes we share communion together in our home. This is similar to how a cell group should function. In fact, the church meeting as a home cell group is a type of spiritual family.

A clan is a group of families that are related. We have come to believe that clusters of cells which relate closely together as a congregation are a type of spiritual clan. The believers in the New Testament church who met from house to house in specific areas were a type of spiritual clan. They were simply an extended spiritual family. For example, according to Romans 16, the believers in Rome met together in homes. But it is also clear that they were in relationship to one another throughout the city.

The third sphere of relationships is that of a spiritual "tribe." For some, this refers to a denomination. For others, it may be a group of churches that work together as a network or as an apostolic fellowship with a common vision. For us, the DOVE Christian Fellowship churches which partner together from various parts of the world represent a spiritual tribe.

The Israelite people consisted of twelve tribes and a multitude of clans and families. They were corporately known as the children of Israel. In the same way, the Lord sees His church as being composed of believers in families, clans and tribes who represent the whole of the kingdom of God.

> For you are all sons of God through faith in Christ Jesus. There is neither Jew nor Greek, there is neither slave nor free, there is neither male nor female; for you are all one in Christ Jesus (Galatians 3:26, 28).

The walls have been broken down! We need one another. I have noticed that when a particular group does not relate to other groups in the body of Christ, in most cases they eventually feel a need to reach out beyond themselves for practical fellowship and accountability. We believe the Lord places this desire in our hearts. Each "tribe" has something to offer the church of Jesus Christ. We must work together. We need each other!

United We Stand

Unity is not created by no longer having denominations or spiritual tribes. Unity comes when believers and leaders of churches, denominations, and networks of churches, can each obey the calling God has given them, while simultaneously affirming the vision God has given to others. Then, as they confirm, support, and pray for one another, the Lord will bless them with tremendous oneness.

It would be foolish for the U.S. Air Force, U.S. Marines, U.S. Army, U.S. Navy and U.S. Coast Guard each to dismantle their area of responsibility and expertise in order to achieve unity. Unity comes as each branch of the military fulfills its responsibilities while maintaining clear communication with the rest of the Armed Forces.

The same principle applies to the church. Let's pursue what the Lord has called us to do with all of our hearts and encourage those in other "spiritual tribes." Let's pray for one another and support each other any way we can. As we do so, Jesus will build His church among us!

I have the privilege of praying on a regular basis with spiritual leaders representing thousands of Christians in our area from different spiritual tribes (denominations). It is tremendous to pray with other servant-leaders in the body of Christ! A few months ago, a group of pastors and other spiritual leaders took some time away to pray, fellowship, learn from one another, and play basketball at a local retreat center. The Lord gave us a tremendous sense of His presence as we spent this time together. The Lord is teaching His church there is no competition in His kingdom!

When the Lord called Gideon to deliver the people of God, Gideon saw himself as an individual member of his family, clan, tribe, and of the Israelite extended family.

> *Then the Lord turned to him and said, "Go in this might of yours, and you shall save Israel from the hand of the*

*Midianites. Have I not sent you?" So he said to Him, "O
my Lord, how can I save Israel? Indeed my clan is the weak-
est in Manasseh, and I am the least in my father's house"
(Judges 6:14-15).*

When Jesus fed the 5000, he saw more than a sea of faces.
He saw individual people and knew that it was most practical
for them to be placed in groups.

*Then He commanded them to make them all sit down in
groups on the green grass. So they sat down in ranks, in
hundreds and in fifties (Mark 6:39-40).*

We are convinced there is a God-ordained need within every man, woman and child to belong to a small group of people
with whom they can relate. In some cases, this need may be
denied due to the hurt and pain of broken or strained past
relationships; however, deep down, the need is still there.

As those who have God-given authority and responsibility for the local church, we have a choice. If we do not provide
the new wineskins (small groups) the Lord ordains, the door
will be open for the devil to form unhealthy groups. The coun-
terfeit will be groups of people who are backbiting and com-
plaining and spreading spiritual cancer throughout the body
or cults which employ the same principle in the service of a
lie. Let's cooperate with the Lord and provide healthy small
groups for God's people so they are not ensnared by the coun-
terfeit.

Understanding Our Terminology

Each fellowship (or body of believers) has its own names
for governmental church structure. So before I go on, I'll take
time to explain the titles we currently use so you can clearly
understand our particular terminology. We must admit that as
a church, we have changed terminology for leaders quite a
few times as we have sought to understand the functions and
roles of leaders and believers.

Our current understanding is that the senior leader of a
church, along with the leadership team, must have a pastor's
heart for the people. However, the primary gifting the Lord
places within a person whom He calls to lead a congregation

(cluster of cells) may not be that of a pastor. It is probably a leadership gift, or an apostolic gift or maybe a combination of various gifts. Perhaps the term "senior elder" and a "team of elders" may be more accurate to describe the senior leader of a congregation and the leadership team.

In this book, we will use the term "senior elder" and "local pastor" interchangeably to describe the one who gives leadership to a local congregation. Even though we often call the senior elder of our congregations a "pastor," we realize that he may not have a pastoral anointing, yet he may have a leadership gift from the Lord to lead the local group of believers. The key is to have another person with a pastoral anointing as a vital part of that leader's team so the people will be cared for pastorally.

The role of the senior elder or local "pastor," then, is to equip believers to do the work of ministry in cell groups. This is quite different from our traditional thinking about the leader of a local church. The image of the pastor in today's church is that of a jack-of-all-trades: He is supposed to be a professional who can preach, visit the sick, balance the church budget, and offer every other type of spiritual service one can think of. In contrast, the focus of local church leadership in the New Testament seems to have been on training the saints for the work of ministry and overseeing that work so the believers could minister effectively in small groups.

Simon and Andrew were fishermen who used nets to catch fish:

> *Then Jesus said to them, "Follow Me, and I will make you become fishers of men" (Mark 1:17).*

One of the "nets" the Lord has given us as we fish for men is cell groups. Since all nets get worn and torn, they must be mended so the fish will not be lost through the holes. Who mends the nets? We believe the majority of net-mending is done by the leadership teams (elders) as they serve local congregations.

The responsibility of the local pastor is not to sit behind a desk. His job is to spend time with the people. He builds (mends) relationships by praying, working, and spending time together with the people he serves. Local pastors go from home to home praying with cell group leaders and section leaders (those who help oversee a small group of cells), helping them to hear from God a strategy for their cell group(s). This helps to assure that there are no holes in the "net," so that no fish are lost, and so that new "fish" can be caught.

The Necessity Of Structure

I've said it before, and you'll hear me say it again: We believe the most practical way for God's people to be encouraged, equipped for the work of ministry, and ministered to is through small groups. An evangelist once told me about a mighty revival which occurred in an area of California during the Jesus Movement of the early 1970s. He returned years later to find only a handful of people still following the Lord. Since there was no spiritual structure to serve and contain the people, no guidelines to follow, no organization and no understanding of spiritual leadership and accountability, many "fell through the cracks." As the Lord brings in the harvest, He wants us to understand spiritual leadership and spiritual structure.

For example, the bones of a physical body provide the structure that is needed to remain healthy as a human being. As we grow, our bones must continue to grow in order to properly facilitate the rest of our body functions. The same principle applies to the Church of Jesus Christ. Our church structures must be constantly changing in order to serve the kingdom of God growing in our midst; however, structure is necessary. Without a bone structure, our body would be a pile of nerves, arteries, muscles and skin lying on the floor. Without an appropriate church structure, the church of Jesus Christ cannot function properly.

In the cell group, the Lord gives the cell leader authority to serve His people. In addition to the Lord's spiritual covering, the cell leader receives spiritual covering from those who delegated to him or her the leadership position (the team of elders from the local congregation).

Sometimes a cell group leader has the gifting to oversee various cells. We call this person a section leader. Usually this section leader will lead his own cell group and oversee a few other cell group leaders. The local pastor works closely with the section leader as he encourages and prays with the cell leaders that are within his realm of responsibility.

When a cell group is ready to multiply, the local pastor gives leadership to the cell multiplication process. The cell group leader and the section leader (if a section leader is a different person from the local pastor) serve with the local pastor during this transition.

This structure also functions very well when individuals in the home cell group are experiencing difficulties or need counsel. For example, if Bob's need is greater than the cell group leader has faith to handle, the section leader or local pastor is there, as one who has grace from the Lord to serve the cell leader and Bob. I want to stress that although this structure works well, it is not to be taken to legalistic extremes. Bob, of course, is free to go to *anyone* for advice, counsel, prayer and fellowship if he feels so led.

During our early years we made the mistake of exercising too much control, and not enough flexibility in this area. For example, if Bob had a problem or struggle, we required him to talk to the cell group leader first before talking to anyone else. Although this was, generally speaking, a good principle to follow, the legalistic manner in which it was carried out was unduly constraining.

Sometimes a person needs to share confidential information but has not yet built enough trust in his relationship with the cell group leader or another person in the cell group. Trust takes time. The ideal situation is for every cell member to have a close enough relationship with other believers in their cell group so they can share about anything, but that is not always the case.

We encourage people within the church to be free to go to anyone they feel they need to go to. Sometimes this may be a professional counselor within or outside our church. Usually if the problem they are facing requires accountability, they will eventually be encouraged to open up their hearts to their cell leader or local pastor. Of course, a trust relationship must be established before they will feel comfortable doing this.

Members of the Body

Every local church has its own criteria regarding membership. I have often been asked the question, "What must I do to become a member of DOVE Christian Fellowship?" Here is what we understand the Bible to say about being a member of the local church.

> *For as the body is one and has many members, but all the members of that one body, being many, are one body, so also is Christ (I Corinthians 12:12).*

The church is called a "body" because everyone is connected somehow to everyone else and together they comprise a single unit. The finger cannot say, "I don't want to be attached to the hand." If it were disconnected, it would no longer have life flowing into it! This would also cause the entire hand to be at a disadvantage because the finger that belongs there is missing.

Membership in the early church was not membership in a club or participation in a meeting. It was practical commitment to Jesus Christ and to individual believers. We believe God wants to bring people into a spiritual family, not merely a weekly service. If a person begins to attend our Sunday morning celebrations but does not show any real interest in cell life, we remind him that, for us, commitment to the body of Christ is not having one's name on a church roll. It is a tangible commitment to be accountable in our Christian walk to a specific group of brothers and sisters in Christ as part of a small group. Attending a Sunday morning service alone limits this person from experiencing the whole scope and thrust of our vision. Church leaders are encouraged to do whatever they can to help this believer find where the Lord is placing him in the body of Christ. (Perhaps it will be in another church in our community.) Of course this person may continue to attend our Sunday celebrations; he will not, however, be able to voice his commitment to our church (become a member) because this is primarily expressed in the cell group setting.

Experiencing church in a small group setting has been wonderful for our family. Although it has been several years since I have had the privilege of serving as a cell group leader (because of my travel schedule in recent years), my family and I are involved in a cell group in our own community. What a tremendous joy it is for our family to serve and be served in this small group setting. We really experience church as a small group of believers. Our seven year old son Josh recently desired to be baptized in water. I phoned our cell leader and the whole cell group went to a local indoor swimming pool where our cell leader and I baptized Josh. "Church" happened right there at the pool!

"What about a missionary or someone who has a job that would keep him away from the cell group meetings?" you may ask. "How can a person like this be committed to a cell group if he or she cannot attend the meetings?" The answer is simple. The meetings are not the issue. The issue is whether or not this believer is wanting to be connected in a living relationship with the other believers in this cell group.

When a young person graduates and goes to college, he is still a vital part of his natural family, although he does not sit down with them at the dinner table every night. The same principle applies to spiritual families in cell groups. There are other ways to keep in contact with a person apart from meeting in a formal setting. Phone calls and letters keep you close to someone who is far away geographically, whether for a short time or longer. Early morning breakfasts and many other get-togethers are possible with someone whose job makes it impossible to meet when the rest of the cell normally gets together.

Biblical Foundations For Every Believer

If a new believer wants to become a part of the local church body, he needs to know what they believe. Every church should have a systematic way of sharing the Scriptures so individuals can understand exactly what they believe. Just as each family has a particular way of doing things, so each church family has various Scriptural understandings and expectations. A church needs to be clear about what its members believe concerning important issues and Biblical doctrines.

During the past few years we have asked every person who came to DOVE Christian Fellowship to take a "Biblical Foundation Course." Anyone who had a desire to be involved as a cell leader or assistant leader was asked first to complete this course as a prerequisite. Cell leaders were also responsible to encourage everyone in their home cell group to complete this course.

The course consisted of twelve 40 minute teachings which were on video cassette. An accompanying notebook served as a study guide and made a good future reference tool. The course was viewed on Sunday mornings at the celebration service, in the home cell group setting, or in an individual's home.

These twelve sessions helped us understand who we were as a church and assisted us in knowing what we believed. Anyone in a cell who had not taken the course was encouraged to do so before expressing commitment to the church in the home group. Viewing these videos periodically as a group, especially when new members came in, was an excellent way to help a new person get established in the cell.

We have now published these twelve Biblical Foundations in twelve separate books. These books, complete with outlines for teaching and questions, are utilized by cell leaders and others to disciple new believers and familiarize those who are new to the church with the basic spiritual principles the Lord has given us as a church family. We have also updated the videos which are used by hundreds of churches worldwide.

In the same way that every family is unique and varied, each church family has its own set of family guidelines. Either a Biblical Foundation Course or a similar substitute will help new persons make a final decision concerning where the Lord may be placing them in the body of Christ.

When a person realizes where God wants him in the body of Christ, he may feel God's call to lead a cell group. What are the qualifications and responsibilities of a cell group leader? How does a leader lead? All these questions and more will be answered in the next three chapters.

Questions to think about from Chapter Four

1. How does the Old Testament pattern for the nation of Israel (family, clan, tribe, etc.) compare to the cell-based church of today?

2. Why do you think Jesus commanded the crowds to sit in groups before He fed them? (See Mark 6:39,40).

3. Why is "structure" necessary in the body of Christ?

4. Contrast structure in the human body with structure in the church body.

CHAPTER 5

AM I QUALIFIED TO BE A CELL GROUP LEADER?

We are all called to go, teach, and disciple the nations, but how can anyone be sure he is specifically called to lead a cell group? If the Lord has put the idea into your heart to lead a cell group, a good place to start is with this attitude, "Lord, I'm willing to begin by serving a few people in my cell, by loving and undergirding them as they fulfill what You have called them to do." If God wants to raise you up for leadership, He'll give you peace, faith and often an anticipation about it in your spirit.

God's basic method of choosing leaders in the Bible was seldom democratic (by popular vote). It was theocratic (by God Himself). When the Lord calls you, you know it in your heart. When God is calling you, the spiritual leadership and the people the Lord has placed around you will also sense the call of God on your life and confirm it. The book of Proverbs tells us that a man's gift makes room for him. Although the literal translation of this scripture speaks of a bribe, an important spiritual principle is implied. When we are gifted by God for a particular task, the people around us will acknowledge that gift and make room for it. It takes time, though, for that to happen:

> *But let these also first be tested; then let them serve as deacons, being found blameless (I Timothy 3:10).*
> *But now God has set the members, each one of them in the body, just as He pleased (I Corinthians 12:18).*

The Scriptures teach us that there is both human and divine affirmation. A leader without the respect of the people he leads may be genuinely called of God but is ineffective until recognized by the people. If there is no confirmation by the people, the timing is probably wrong. He needs to wait prayerfully for further instructions from the Lord, trusting God to open and close doors and reveal His will both to him and others.

Cell Group Leading—Pursuing The Call

I, therefore, the prisoner of the Lord, beseech you to walk worthy of the calling with which you were called (Ephesians 4:1).

It is a real privilege to be called by the Lord to serve His people as a cell group leader or assistant leader. It's also encouraging to know the Lord calls average people like you and me. Remember, many of His disciples were common fishermen. The call to cell group ministry is a holy calling and is not to be taken lightly. Leading a cell group is a vital work in the body of Christ, and it offers the wonderful reward of seeing lives changed by the power of the Holy Spirit!

In Philippians 3:14, Paul responded to new areas God was leading him into by saying, "I press toward the goal for the prize of the upward call of God in Christ Jesus." This is the attitude we need to have as we sense God calling us to lead a cell group.

Qualifications For A Cell Group Leader

The most important thing a cell group leader or assistant leader needs to know is that God has called him to that work. The cell leader has received authority from the Lord and from the local leadership who have acknowledged and appointed him. In addition to being assured of his call, it is crucial that a cell leader has a heart of humility toward those whom he is serving. A test as to whether or not he has passed this requirement is very simple. Has this leader been willing to serve under someone else's leadership, especially someone he hasn't always agreed with? If he has, he will probably have the grace that is needed to lead with humility.

We believe one does not need to be a Bible College graduate to fulfill the requirements of leading a cell group. The best kind of leader is simply one who is willing to be a servant to God's people in the cell and share with them the love of Jesus Christ. Cell group leaders serve the believers in the cell group in practical ways and also encourage them to hear from God and trust Him to meet their needs. Our availability is often more useful to God than our ability.

If someone comes to our church from a Bible College and has the training and knowledge to lead, it does not mean he or she is immediately qualified to be a cell group leader. We believe it is important to give a person time to serve in a cell group before he is entrusted with the greater responsibility of leading a home cell group.

In business, the manager who is often most effective in giving leadership to a company is the one who actually has experience in the particular field. That person knows the "ins and outs" of such work, and the problems and challenges that will be faced. The same is true in the church.

This vital truth needs to be balanced with a proper understanding of God's grace and servanthood. If not, it can lead to a performance mentality and selfish ambition. This is accepted in the business world but is obviously unacceptable in the church.

A true leader has a servant's heart and is willing to take the time needed to be "knit with" the people in his cell. Ephesians tells us,

> . . . *from whom the whole body, joined and knit together by what every joint supplies, according to the effective working by which every part does its share, causes growth of the body for the edifying of itself in love (Ephesians 4:16).*

If I were to break a bone, it would take several weeks for the bone to heal and be knit together. The church is built by relationships. It takes time for relationships to be knit together.

Cell Leaders Need To Have A Clear Testimony

> *For this reason I also suffer these things; nevertheless I am not ashamed, for I know whom I have believed and am*

persuaded that He is able to keep what I have committed to Him until that Day (II Timothy 1:12).

If you are called to be a leader, you must have a clear testimony about your salvation, water baptism, and baptism in the Holy Spirit. Areas of healing and deliverance which you have personally experienced should also be part of your testimony.

Tell your own story to your cell group with a sense of expectancy that God will use it to build faith in His people. Not only is faith built, but often God's Spirit will move, and people will be bound together in a special way after candid testimonies are shared. After one cell leader shared his testimony, a woman, new to the cell, and sensing God's compassion and love in the room, broke down and sobbed as she revealed the pain of giving up her child for adoption as a young pregnant teenager. Cell members were able to put their arms around her as God healed those emotions she had buried deep inside for years. It all started with a cell leader simply sharing freely how God had saved, healed and delivered him of hurts in the past.

Leaders should also be able to share how God is continuously working in their lives on an ongoing basis. They should have a testimony that is current because of the vital relationship they have with Jesus Christ.

Cell Leaders Need To Be Full Of Faith

Cell leaders must be people who are full of faith and full of the Holy Spirit. Stephen was known as a man with these qualities.

And the saying pleased the whole multitude. And they chose Stephen, a man full of faith and the Holy Spirit . . . (Acts 6:5).

As a home cell group leader, you will need to exercise your faith by using your spiritual gifts as well. How can a leader help someone else experience spiritual gifts if he does not exercise those gifts himself? For example, if the leader is not hospitable, many times the people in the home cell group will not learn the importance of hospitality. If the leader doesn't share his experience about being baptized in the Holy Spirit, the believers in the home cell group will not think it is very important to be baptized with the Holy Spirit. If the leaders do not prophesy and exercise spiritual gifts, the people in the home cell group probably will not prophesy or exercise spiritual gifts either.

We speak what we know, but we impart who we are. If you find yourself lacking in some of these areas, talk to your local pastor or another confidant. They can lead you to someone who has a special anointing in the area you are lacking. "Anointing comes by association," as the saying goes. Spend time with a person who has the particular anointing you desire to grow in, and expect the Lord to use you in the same way. That's what faith is all about.

As a young Christian, I had an intense desire to see the Lord move supernaturally. I saw so many people in bondage who needed to be set free, yet I often felt helpless to do anything about it. I knew the Bible said that Jesus Christ is the same yesterday, today, and forever, but I seldom saw the Lord manifest His power in a supernatural way. I then met some friends who were experiencing the Lord's power at work. People were delivered from demons and set free from the oppression of the enemy. I began to spend time with these friends. I watched and prayed as they ministered to others. Before long I was experiencing in my own life the same power that comes through the name of Jesus. Young men and women who came to me for help were being set free.

Cell Leaders Need To Support
The Vision Of The Local Church

All families do things differently, and we need to be convinced that the vision of our church is one we can embrace as our own so we can enthusiastically carry out our part in its fulfillment. This is why we encourage all cell leaders to be well acquainted with our Biblical Foundation Course, so they clearly understand the mandate the Lord has given to us.

There are probably no two believers on the face of the earth who agree about everything. If there is any aspect of the ministry of a church that a home cell group leader cannot consent to or support in faith, he should "share his heart" with his local leadership. We need to appeal to those over us in the Lord when we are having difficulty with an area in our lives or in the life of the church. Many times the Lord will use our appeal to authority to bring change in an area of the church that needs modification.

If a leader is rebellious or divisive, he cannot display the kind of loyalty toward his church that the people need to see exhibited.

> *Now I plead with you, brethren, by the name of our Lord Jesus Christ, that you all speak the same thing, and that there be no divisions among you, but that you be perfectly joined together in the same mind and in the same judgment (I Corinthians 1:10).*

A lack of loyalty to the Word of God and to the local church will cause great harm to the sheep. Some will be confused and others may even scatter to seek other leaders because of their confusion. Sometimes new believers may get involved in cults and deception because of the influence of "more mature" Christians who sowed seeds of doubt about their local church or its leadership.

If you are serving as a cell group leader and you find yourself having a wrong spirit toward those in spiritual leadership over you, you need to ask the Lord for grace to correct your attitude immediately. If you cannot seem to find freedom, then sit down with your leaders and share your struggle. When we confess our faults one to another and pray for one another, we can receive healing in these areas (James 5:16).

The Scripture tells us that whatever we sow, we shall also reap (Galatians 6:7). We will find people under our spiritual care responding to us in the same way we have responded to those who are over us in the Lord. If we are loyal, others will be loyal to us. If we have a wrong attitude, people under our spiritual care will have the same type of attitude.

Just because our opinion differs with another person in leadership over a certain situation does not mean we are rebellious or that we cannot remain loyal. God wants us to pray about the difference of understanding we have and then talk about it with the appropriate leadership He has placed in our lives.

I've been thankful for the many times believers in the church have shared areas in which they thought we should change as a church. Some of these ideas were implemented and brought great blessing to our church. It is much easier for a person in authority to receive input from one who has prayed and has a teachable spirit. It is spiritually healthy for us to appeal to the authorities God has placed in our lives.

A Cell Leader Needs To Be Personable And Easy To Approach

Cell group leaders must learn to be "people oriented." A leader's attitude should be, "I will lay down my life to see the believers in our cell group become men and women of God." Matthew Henry, in his famous commentary on the Bible, says, "Those whose business it is to instruct people in the affairs of their souls should be humble, mild, and easy of access." A good leader cannot think, "I'll lead the meeting and teach the Bible, but then I don't want to be bothered all week with anyone's problems." That cell group is destined to die. Leaders must always be of the attitude, "I'm here to help!"

Remember you are not called to do everything. Learn to delegate. People learn best by doing. The goal of every cell leader should be to work himself out of a job as others' talents and gifts are multiplied.

The cell group leader should primarily be a facilitator, rather than the person who is doing everything. Perhaps you could write down the different roles and responsibilities needed for the cell to function effectively. Then ask each cell member to pray about how their gifts might be used in carrying out these various areas of responsibility.

Ask people in your home cell group questions in order to gain insights into how they feel about your cell group and about your leadership. Some questions you may ask are, "If you were me, what would you do differently?" "How can I better serve you?" "What areas in your life can I pray with you about?"

Home Cell Leaders Should Be Enthusiastic

It is vitally important that you genuinely care for the people in your cell group and are enthusiastic about serving them.

Your enthusiasm to serve Jesus and others will rub off on those in your group.

Pastor Cho says that the first qualification of a cell leader is to be enthusiastic about the things of God. Enthusiasm is contagious. People want to follow someone who leads energetically. They will sense that God's work is important to you when they see you putting your whole heart into it. The Bible says,

> *And whatever you do, do it heartily, as to the Lord and not to men (Colossians 3:23).*

We are commanded by the Lord to do everything with enthusiasm! An enthusiastic leader will produce enthusiastic Christians in his cell group.

Cell Leaders Should Be Gifted to Lead People and Recognize Others with that Gift

Where do hurting sheep go? They go to a shepherd. Just as sheep follow shepherds, people are naturally drawn to those in the church who have a genuine gift of leadership. As a home cell group leader, God will supply you with all the grace and gifting that you will need to carry out what He has called you to do.

Home cell group leaders need to be constantly on the lookout for others in their cell group with a gift of leadership. If you notice that people are attracted to Sarah because she genuinely cares about them and serves them faithfully, encourage those qualities in Sarah. Ask the Lord if He may be instructing you to ask Sarah if she would pray about being an assistant leader of your cell in the future. God may eventually call her to lead a cell group after she receives on-the-job training.

A Home Cell Leader Should Not be a Novice

> *. . . not a novice, lest being puffed up with pride he fall into the same condemnation as the devil (I Timothy 3:6).*

A new Christian should not be a cell group leader, because he needs time and experience before being entrusted with taking care of others. A leader cannot be a new convert to Christianity, in the same way a one-year-old child cannot be a baby-sitter. Elisha was trained by Elijah. Timothy was trained by Paul. In each case, the training took a reasonable amount of time. In the business world, workers and executives alike receive training before assuming responsibility. In the church, local leadership is responsible to discern when someone is trained and ready to lead. Each case will be different.

One possibility for new Christians who want to serve in leadership is to have them start as assistant cell leaders. In this role they are essentially "leaders in training." Right in the cell group they can get the practical, hands-on training they'll need to help them grow.

When an assistant is learning during this apprenticeship period, he or she must be allowed to fail. As home group leaders, we must remember that we, too, made mistakes as we progressed through the learning process. If we do not forget what we went through as we matured, we will not be tempted to adopt unreasonable expectations for the cell leaders that come after us. As cell leaders, our goal should be to support our assistant leader(s) in success and failure alike and to continue to train them in love.

Married Cell Leaders Need to be in Unity with Their Spouses About Their Decision to Lead a Cell Group

It's important that leading a cell group does not cause disunity in a marriage. The spouse should not only confirm his or her partner's call to serve, but if possible, should be actively engaged in serving the group also.

The Scriptures affirm that God uses both men and women as home cell group leaders in the church. Priscilla and Aquila worked together as a team in the New Testament (Romans 16:3). It is possible that she was giving leadership to the people God placed within her spiritual care, while her husband supported her.

Many times we have seen the Lord use women in a leadership role in the home group setting, while their husbands play a supporting role. Cell leaders Ken and Kim are a married couple having roles like this. Kim, the more verbal of the two, bubbles with enthusiasm and is gifted in teaching and hospitality. She usually leads the cell meetings, plans activities, teaches and generally keeps things rolling. Ken is quiet and prefers to work behind the scenes. A compassionate man, he opens his heart and house to those in the cell and is always available to lend a helping hand or to pray with someone. This husband and wife team complement each other and flow together in unity.

When a potential cell leader has a spouse who is unsaved, it is best for the spouse to confirm his or her involvement in leadership. In certain situations where the unsaved spouse is antagonistic toward the Lord and His Church, the potential cell leader will find great wisdom in praying with other spiritual leaders in the church to discern the mind of the Lord before he or she begins to lead a cell.

If a couple is newly married, please note that leading a cell group is an added responsibility. Some newlyweds may not be ready for this ministry, while others may be prepared to serve in this way.

Cell Leaders are Encouraged
to Tithe to the Local Church

"Bring all the tithes into the storehouse, that there may be food in My house, and try Me now in this," says the Lord of hosts, "If I will not open for you the windows of heaven and pour out for you such blessing that there will not be room enough to receive it" (Malachi 3:10).

The storehouse is the place where God's people bring their tithes and offerings. A tithe is 10% of our income. This is a part of God's plan to supply the needs of the leadership, the paid workers of the local church, and missionaries that are sent throughout the world.

Wherever we invest our money is where our true interests lie. "For where your treasure is, there your heart will be also" (Matthew 6:21). Our hearts need to be in our local church, including our own cell group. We need to support it with our money and our time.

Whether or not we give our tithe to the local church is a clear barometer of our commitment to the local church where we are placed. It is easy to say we are committed to the church, but if we are not willing to tithe to the "storehouse," we probably need to reconsider the depth of this commitment.

Some people believe tithing is an Old Testament practice that is not observed in the New Testament. Jesus speaks of tithing clearly in Matthew chapter 23, verse 23:

> *Woe to you, scribes and Pharisees, hypocrites! For you pay tithe of mint and anise and cumin, and have neglected the weightier matters of the law: justice and mercy and faith. These you ought to have done, without leaving the others undone (Matthew 23:23).*

If cell group leaders are not tithing to their own local church, they find it very difficult to teach this Biblical principle with conviction to those in their cell group, since they are not applying it to their own lives. We do not tithe out of obligation or because of the law, but out of the desire of our hearts to be obedient to the Lord, and in order to see His church advance.

Cell Leaders Need to be Accountable

> *Obey those who rule over you, and be submissive, for they watch out for your souls, as those who must give account. Let them do so with joy and not with grief, for that would be unprofitable for you (Hebrews 13:17).*

What is accountability? The word *accountability* literally means *to give an account.* In our own individual lives, we are accountable to the Lord regarding how we live out our commitment to Christ. Our lives need to "line up" with the Word of God. Personal accountability is not having others tell us what to do. Personal accountability is finding out from God what He wants us to do and then asking others to "hold us accountable" to those things.

Many times I have asked others to approach me about "giving an account" to them regarding a goal I believe the Lord set for me. Several years ago, I asked one of the men in our cell group to hold me accountable with my personal time in prayer and in meditating on God's Word each day. Every morning at 7:00 AM I received a phone call as my friend checked up on me. Accountability enabled me to be victorious.

Sometimes we are held accountable for responsibilities that have been delegated to us by others whom the Lord has placed over us. For instance, employees are held accountable by their employers. In the New Testament, Paul the Apostle held those churches whose foundations he had labored to establish, accountable to continue to build on Jesus Christ. Paul expected the leaders of these churches to "give an account" to himself and to the Lord for the way they were living their lives. Since the cell leader is an extension of the leadership of the local church, the cell leader is accountable to the leadership the Lord has placed in His church.

One way for us to discern whether or not we are planted properly in the body of Christ is to ask ourselves this question: Is it a joy to be accountable to the Lord and to our spiritual leaders for our Christian walk and for the way we serve in our local expression of the body of Christ? If being accountable to our local spiritual leaders is burdensome, we may be improperly placed in the body of Christ.

True accountability consists in someone loving us enough to check up on us, to see how we are doing in our personal lives and how those in our cell group are doing spiritually and relationally. I am grateful when those the Lord has placed in my life ask me about my relationship with my wife and children, or hold me accountable for my prayer life—it helps to keep me on track.

The leadership team of the local church is ultimately responsible before the Lord for each person in the cell groups. The cell leader, then, is an extension of the leadership team of the local church. According to the Scriptures, the elders in the local church "give an account" to the Lord for those under their spiritual oversight. Cell group leaders serve and assist the elders by ministering to God's people within the cell group over which they have charge.

It is important for the cell group leader to converse regularly and to pray with those whom the Lord has placed over him. In this way, he is being accountable for his particular area of service and the well-being of those in his cell group. Accountability is one of the greatest protections God has given us individually and as a church. Each one who is called into leadership in the body of Christ needs to be accountable to the Lord and to the servant leaders He has established in His church. The senior leader of each local church and the leadership team he represents need to be accountable for their actions, not only to the Lord, but to others in the body of Christ. This accountability may be to other leaders in the denomination or "apostolic fellowship" to which the church he represents is connected. Or, he may be accountable to other church leaders in his community. Better yet, he may be accountable to both.

The Kind of People God Calls to Leadership

Let's take a look at the kind of people God calls into leadership. This may surprise you! Let's start with Moses:

> *Come now, therefore, and I will send you to Pharaoh that you may bring My people, the children of Israel, out of Egypt. But Moses said to God, "Who am I that I should go to Pharaoh, and that I should bring the children of Israel out of Egypt?" So He said, "I will certainly be with you . . . "* *(Exodus 3:10-12).*

Moses was basically saying, "Who am I?" Most leaders feel this way when the Lord calls them to any type of leadership. The first time I was ever asked to pray publicly, I read my prayer off a piece of scratch paper. I was scared! The first small group I led seemed like a monumental task! But I took a step of faith. Joshua did too.

> *Have I not commanded you? Be strong and of good courage; do not be afraid, nor be dismayed, for the Lord your God is with you wherever you go (Joshua 1:9).*

The Lord had to encourage Joshua continually in his new role as a leader. We do not depend on our ability but upon His ability in us! Gideon also struggled with the Lord's call to leadership in His life:

> *Gideon said to Him, "O my lord, if the Lord is with us, why then has all this happened to us? And where are all His miracles which our fathers told us about, saying, 'Did not the Lord bring us up from Egypt?' But now the Lord has forsaken us and delivered us into the hands of the Midianites." Then the Lord turned to him and said, "Go in*

> *this might of yours, and you shall save Israel from the hand*
> *of the Midianites. Have I not sent you?" So he said to Him,*
> *"O my Lord, how can I save Israel? Indeed my clan is the*
> *weakest in Manasseh, and I am the least in my father's*
> *house." And the Lord said to him, "Surely I will be with*
> *you, and you shall defeat the Midianites as one man" (Judges*
> *6:13-16).*

Jeremiah felt the same way many youth cell group leaders feel when they begin to lead a cell group:

> *Then said I: "Ah, Lord God! Behold, I cannot speak, for I*
> *am a youth." But the Lord said to me: "Do not say, 'I am a*
> *youth,' for you shall go to all to whom I send you, and what-*
> *ever I command you, you shall speak. Do not be afraid of*
> *their faces, for I am with you to deliver you," says the Lord*
> *(Jeremiah 1:6-8).*

Each of these men felt a profound sense of inadequacy when the Lord called them to leadership. That is the type of person the Lord seeks to use—those who are completely dependent on Him! According to the Bible, God delights in manifesting His strength through the weak. In II Corinthians 12:9 the Lord tells us, ". . . for my strength is made perfect in weakness."

We must be convinced that if God doesn't show up, it is all over! So if you feel like you may be called to cell group leadership or to church leadership within any sphere, but you don't think you have all the natural gifts you need, or feel you have made too many mistakes, be encouraged—you are in good company!

Remember, man looks at the outward appearance, but the Lord looks at the heart. When our heart is in the right place, in complete submission to Him, it is amazing what the Lord can do to prepare and equip us for the responsibilities that lie ahead.

Questions to think about
from Chapter Five

1. Comment on the statement: "Our availability is often more useful to God than our ability."

2. What are the characteristics of a "servant's heart"?

3. Why is it important for everyone in the cell group to share their testimony and practice their spiritual gifts?

4. What are your spiritual gifts? Do you use your spiritual gifts in any small group setting?

5. If you are a cell leader, to whom are you accountable?

6. What was the characteristic response of the men God called to leadership in the Bible (Moses, Gideon and Jeremiah)?

CHAPTER 6

THE RESPONSIBILITIES OF A CELL GROUP LEADER

The challenge that the Lord has set before us is to know Him, to reach the lost, and to make disciples. This is the basic job description of a cell group leader. In accepting the responsibility to encourage and serve a small group of believers, our first priority (next to maintaining a close relationship with Jesus and serving our families) is to pray for those the Lord has placed in our home cell group.

Cell Leaders Are Responsible To Pray

> *So I sought for a man among them who would make a wall, and stand in the gap before Me on behalf of the land, that I should not destroy it; but I found no one (Ezekiel 22:30).*

God has called us to "stand in the gap" for both the saved and the unsaved. We are called to pray for people in our cell group. Since we are encouraged in Scripture to "pray without ceasing," I believe the Lord would be pleased if we purposed in our hearts to "cover" each person in our cell group daily in prayer. We should also pray specifically for family members, friends, and acquaintances of those in our cell who are unsaved. Some of my friends in New Zealand call the unsaved "pre-Christians." I like that. There is faith in that kind of terminology.

Praying is hard work. Like anything else worthwhile, it must be learned, and learning takes time!

My little children, for whom I labor in birth again until Christ is formed in you . . . (Galatians 4:19).

One of the greatest ways to serve those within the home cell group is to "labor in prayer" for them. Ask God for direction and He will show you how to pray diligently for each person.

Assuredly, I say to you, whatever you bind on earth will be bound in heaven, and whatever you loose on earth will be loosed in heaven (Matthew 18:18).

You also need to be involved in spiritual warfare on a daily basis. God has given you the authority to bind the powers of evil and to loose blessing and freedom in the name of Jesus! When praying for the people for whom we are spiritually responsible, it is important that we pray in Jesus' name against any divisive spirits that would try to hinder our home cell group.

For we do not wrestle against flesh and blood, but against principalities, against powers, against the rulers of the darkness of this age, against spiritual hosts of wickedness in the heavenly places (Ephesians 6:12).

Many people don't know they are being manipulated by demonic spirits. When people are manipulated by demonic spirits, they may simply seem disinterested or unresponsive to what is going on in the cell group. In reality, the enemy is hindering them. As a cell leader, you need to "get in your prayer closet" and pray for them in Jesus' name, taking authority over those spirits that are holding them back.

If someone is struggling with a life-controlling problem or openly displaying demonic activity, it is usually best for the cell leaders to meet with this person outside of the cell meeting. This will give opportunity for further prayer, counsel, ministry and deliverance. In areas of deliverance from demonic spirits, it is best to minister two by two whenever possible.

I met a friend in a restaurant one day who was struggling with a habit of smoking cigarettes. He hated it, but seemed unable to stop. He was not free to share with the whole group of people in his cell, but he was open with me when we were alone. I prayed for him in the restaurant and he asked me to take his cigarettes and destroy them. I instructed him to confess the Scripture, "sin (cigarettes) shall have no dominion over me" (Romans 6:14). During the next few weeks I checked in on him and encouraged him to continue to trust the Word of God. He was set free. II Corinthians 10:3,4 says,

> *For though we walk in the flesh, we do not war according to the flesh. For the weapons of our warfare are not carnal but mighty in God for pulling down strongholds.*

As you serve the people in prayer behind the scenes, your group will experience more unity of spirit and a better atmosphere for spiritual growth.

Praying the Scriptures has been a helpful way for me to pray. When you pray the Word of God, you can know that you are praying the Lord's will. Personalize Scripture with the names of those for whom you are praying. For example: "I pray that (Brian's) love may abound more and more . . . " (Philippians 1:9-11). Other excellent "Scripture prayers" to use in praying for spiritual growth among those in your cell group can be found in Colossians 1:9-12, Ephesians 1:15-21, and Ephesians 3:14-19.

As believers in Jesus Christ, we can pray with confidence that the Father hears us and will answer our prayers. Philippians 1:6 teaches us to be "confident of this very thing, that He who has begun a good work in you will complete it until the day of Jesus Christ." We should pray this truth for those in our cell group and for those the Lord is drawing into His kingdom.

I could give countless illustrations of times when cell members have agreed together in prayer for someone, and God has moved sovereignly to draw that person to Himself. I like to tell the story of two new Christians, Jim and Julie, who began to pray with their cell group for the salvation of Jim's father. For years, this man had been angered by any mention of God or religion, but after this group began to pray, Jim noticed that his father began to show an inquisitive attitude toward God. Jim knew the prayers of the saints were not going unnoticed. Then Jim's dad had a terrible accident. In the last hours of his life, while he was still conscious and in a clear-minded state, a nun at the hospital led Jim's dad to Jesus. Although it was difficult to see a loved one die, Jim and Julie were able to rejoice along with their cell group because they knew that the prayers of cell members had played a part in bringing Jim's dad out of the kingdom of darkness and into the kingdom of light.

As a leader you must set the standard in prayer. Some time ago, I asked the Lord how to have a church that prays. He spoke clearly and said, "You pray." It's important to have someone to pray with whenever possible. Jesus said in Matthew 18:19:

I say to you that if two of you agree on earth concerning anything that they ask, it will be done for them by My Father in heaven.

Pray with your assistant leader on a regular basis. This will help to alert you both to any problems that may accompany the spiritual growth that is occurring in your cell group. Pray with your section leader or with your local pastor. It is important that you pray regularly with your pastors and those who have been placed over you by the Lord.

Some cell groups find it helpful for each person in the cell to have a prayer partner. This may be changed monthly or from time to time. Prayer teams for spiritual warfare are also effective. Small group prayer is important because it helps us to know the heart of others; this fosters spiritual intimacy and strengthens relationships. Remember to pray with expectancy! Through doubt and unbelief, the enemy will try to break our communication line to God.

If your cell group seems to be lacking in the area of prayer, have someone come into your cell group who has an anointing in the area of prayer. Prayer is contagious. As you pray with someone who has a "spirit of intercession," your entire cell group will begin to experience power in prayer. Praying together will also help bring unity to the cell group.

Cell Leaders are Called to Encourage, Not to Control

One of the lessons to be learned from history is that cell leaders who are immature or insecure may seek to control God's people rather than encourage them to hear from the Lord for themselves. Our goal must be to present every believer mature in Christ.

> *Him we preach, warning every man and teaching every man in all wisdom, that we may present every man perfect in Christ Jesus (Colossians 1:28).*

We need to help the believers in our cell learn how to receive direction from the Lord themselves, not encourage them to depend on us by telling them what to do. For example, in considering questions of family finances, family size, child rearing styles, political differences, decisions about standard of living and so on, a cell leader can give counsel based on his understanding of the Word of God, but issues not clearly decided by Scripture must ultimately be left to the conscience of each believer.

Dr. Cho, in his book *Successful Home Cell Groups*, gives some excellent advice on this subject:

> *In the past, many home groups have been established outside of the local church and outside of established denominations . . . In some cases these independent groups led many Christians into bondage. No one could make a decision unless it was confirmed by the elders of the group. Personal communication with the Holy Spirit was discouraged as those in authority began to exercise greater control over the personal lives of the members, including telling them who they should marry and telling younger members if they were permitted to have contact with their "unbelieving" parents. One of the problems with the independent home groups is that some of them have exercised too much control over their members. That is wrong. In our church the cell leaders are there to help oversee the spiritual growth of the members, and to encourage them in fellowship and evangelism. But they are never to meddle in the affairs of the members. That is not the responsibility of the church. Each member must be encouraged and taught to depend on the Holy Spirit himself and to develop a life of faith. I never encourage our members to become dependent on the cell leaders, because that would be as bad as communism or the Moonies. Anything that destroys personal independence and the individual's personality and responsibility is from the devil. God never created us to be puppets. He gave us personalities to be developed into loving sons and daughters living in relationship with Him. Our home cell groups are designed to promote that relationship. [8]*

The Cell Leader's Leadership
is Limited in Four Ways:

1. He cannot deviate in any way from Scripture and still retain his spiritual leadership. (Believers should go to God's Word first to see what God is saying to them before they take the cell leader's word for it.)

2. He cannot act contrary to the values and guiding principles set by the leadership team of the church in which He serves and still retain his spiritual leadership.

3. He cannot assume the guiding role of the Holy Spirit in the life of another believer. Every believer must ultimately hear from God for himself.

4. He cannot misuse his role of leadership by being abusive, manipulative, or self-serving in any way (for example, by expecting a return for his investment into the lives of people, whether financial, physical or psychological).

Section Leader—
A Cell Leader Who Oversees Several Cells

We call a cell leader who leads his own cell and is also gifted and graced to oversee several other cell leaders, a "section leader." A section leader usually is responsible for approximately 2-6 cell groups. Many times the cell groups that a section leader oversees have been birthed out of the cell group that he leads. In this case, the relationships have already been established between the section leader and the cell leaders he is responsible for. A job description for a section leader would include praying daily for the cell group leaders he oversees and meeting with the cell group leaders for prayer and encouragement as needed. A section leader also encourages the cell groups within their section to come together for outreach—fellowship, picnics, teaching, etc. as the Holy Spirit leads. They serve the local pastors by sharing their experiences as a cell group leader and clearly communicating their spiritual insights with the cell group leaders for whom they are responsible.

Cell Leaders Need To Be
Trained and Need To Train Assistants

Our church has prepared a "Cell Group Leaders' Training Course" for each potential cell leader to complete before he begins leading a cell group. We also have cell leaders' training days which are usually held a few times each year on a Saturday with various workshops and training sessions for small group leaders. In addition, training is provided at monthly cell leaders' meetings, some of which are held on the local congregation level. Others are held on a church-wide level. New and ongoing matters concerning the church-wide body are communicated when all of the cell group leaders in the whole church come together for a time of training and encouragement. This *House to House* manual is also used to serve as a resource for local pastors to train new cell group leaders. For example, we have utilized this book as a five week training course for present and future cell group leaders. We call it, "Back to the Basics."

However, the best training is still the one-on-one training that takes place when a potential cell leader is discipled by his cell leader or the assistant cell leader. The most effective training is on-the-job-training. Go along with a cell leader when he goes into the hospital to pray for the sick, or join him when he meets with someone who is discouraged and prays a prayer of faith for him. It has always been a joy for me to lead others to Christ as another believer joins with me as an apprentice and a prayer partner. This way he can witness the miracle of a new birth right before his eyes. Jesus set the pattern for on-the-job-training. He spent most of his time training a few men, not teaching great crowds. God wants us to train others to train others, to train others . . .

My friend John still talks about the times he joined me witnessing to people in a local park. We walked through the park and took a step of faith in obedience to the Lord as He led us to share the gospel with certain individuals. Although I was totally unaware of it at the time, this was a life changing experience for John.

Cell leaders in training need to understand clearly the Scriptural principles they learn from training courses, as well as from on-the-job-training. They will need to be grounded in the Word in order to teach others. Practically speaking, it is best for a future cell leader to be regularly involved in cell group functions, in weekly celebration meetings, and in personal ministry in the small group setting before beginning to minister as a cell leader.

It is also important to be organized, perhaps using an appointment book, or some other type of daily reminder to help remember appointments and to arrive on time. To continue to forget an appointment with someone gives them the impression that we don't really care.

At the start of a new cell, the cell leader should pray for at least one or more assistant leader(s) to serve with him in the home group. Several assistants can be trained at the same time or over a period of time. A scriptural method for training, whether it be for leading people to Christ or church leadership, is found in II Timothy 2:2,

> And the things that you have heard from me among many witnesses, commit these to faithful men who will be able to teach others also.

The home cell group becomes the basic training center for all kinds of ministry. Missionaries do not suddenly and miraculously become trained overnight and leave for foreign fields. They get training and practice in their home cell group. Job training for leadership must include a hands-on situation. The first qualities to look for in an assistant are those of faithfulness, humility, and the willingness to serve.

Throughout the past few years we have found that there are three basic types of assistant leaders in cell groups: developmental assistant leaders, perpetual assistant leaders, and catalyst assistant leaders. Here is a brief definition for each type of assistant leader.

1. Developmental—those being trained for future leadership. Jesus had twelve assistants, but He seemed to be training Peter as His chief assistant.

2. Perpetual—someone who is not a potential leader; however, when a home cell group multiplies, this assistant leader gives a sense of stability and continuity to one of the new cells. When the cell multiplies into two, this person(s) often becomes an assistant leader in one of these new cells. This person may always serve in a supportive role and not ever be called to be a cell group leader.

3. Catalyst—someone in church leadership; a person who has a "fivefold ministry gift" or a person who serves as a supported staff person in the church who is a part of your cell. This person may not be able to take an active role in cell leadership due to traveling ministry or the responsibility to minister at other cells. However, this person will prove to be very supportive to the cell leader and will be a good resource and example of Christ's love within the cell group.

Process of Confirming New Assistant Leaders

When a cell leader senses that a certain person in the cell (let's say Betty) would make a great assistant leader, he should initially communicate with his section leader about the possibility of adding a new assistant to help with cell group responsibilities. When it is clear after prayer that Betty would be a wise choice, Betty is asked to pray about the possibility of being involved in leadership in the future. After Betty is assured that God is calling her, and there is a sense of confirmation from the home cell group, a commissioning service should be planned. Betty is commissioned through the laying on of hands, with prayer to God from the cell group members, the section leader, and the local church leadership. If the section leader or any of the local pastors cannot be involved in the commissioning, it is advantageous for those who are absent to make personal contact with Betty to affirm her in her new role.

Assistant Cell Leader's
Responsibility to the Cell Leader

Betty's new responsibility as an assistant leader not only involves praying with, but also for, the cell leader to encourage him in his call. She will serve the cell leader in any way she can so that the home group is a successful one—that is, one in which people are coming to Christ and being discipled. In the absence of the leader, she will give leadership to the group and look for ways to assist the leader by praying for and with people, discipling, encouraging, and serving in practical ways. An assistant leader will also bring to the cell leader's attention areas of concern: potential problems, needs or "blind spots."

Assistant Cell Leader's
Responsibility to Those in the Cell

In addition to serving her cell group leader, Betty, the assistant, will diligently pray for those in her cell group. She will help the cell leader to contact individuals regularly by phone or in person to comfort, strengthen, and encourage them, giving special oversight and time to the one(s) they are discipling. Some practical ways of serving may include providing rides to meetings as needed, giving cell group information to cell members, and giving special care to new believers.

Having a Pastor's Heart

During the early years of DOVE Christian Fellowship, we called each cell leader the "pastor" of his cell group. We have come to believe it was a mistake to do that. A cell leader always must be willing to serve those in his cell group through prayer, encouragement and relationship; however, he may or may not have the gifting of a pastor. Some cell leaders are gifted administrators, others are evangelists, others are teachers, and so on.

When we called cell group leaders "pastors," some of them got overwhelmed and quit. Others, because of their traditional understanding of the word "pastor," felt like they should have a ministerial license to be a cell group leader.

We believe we should call the cell leaders what they really are. If they are cell leaders, then we should call them that. In actuality, a cell leader seems to be serving in a deacon-type role. Deacons are ministers (servants to the body of Christ). If we see them as cell shepherds, then we should call them that. We just need to be sure that the terminology that is used is clearly articulating the vision that the Lord has given to us.

Again, the home cell group leader is not expected to be the pastor. He may have some pastoral gifting, but should only respond to situations according to his measure of faith. Some home group leaders have a pastoral gift within them and perhaps will be used as pastors with greater spiritual responsibilities in the future.

On the other hand, every cell leader needs to have a pastor's heart. A person with a pastor's heart has a desire to serve a group of people through prayer, regular encouragement, and practical service, although it does not mean he has the final pastoral responsibility.

A teenager might "mother" her younger brother or sister, but that does not make her the true mother. Later on, she will be a mother and have her own children. This same principle applies to those who are "pastoring" as cell leaders. Cell leaders are serving alongside the local pastors and others in leadership in their local area so that every saint can and will be involved in the work of ministry.

Set the Example

In the cell group setting, the enemy will lie to us at times and tell us that we cannot really help others because we have not "been there." Was Jesus ever on drugs or alcohol? Was He ever divorced? No, of course not, yet He has set our example. Regardless of our backgrounds, we can pray and trust the living God and see the Lord do miracles among us.

You can set the example by sharing your own personal needs and problems with those in your cell group. The Bible tells us in II Corinthians 12:9 that we should boast in our weaknesses so that the power of Christ may rest upon us. When we are open about areas of struggle that we've had and share how the Lord has given us grace to conquer by His Word, it causes us to be transparent. This keeps us from being placed upon a pedestal. When people put us on a pedestal, we open ourselves to the enemy in the area of pride. People we are serving feel as though they can never attain our level of spirituality, which is totally untrue.

We can minister most effectively by showing the people in our cell group the Word of God rather than by giving them our own opinions. If you don't have the answer, don't fake it. Tell them honestly that you don't know, but you will find the answer. That's why God provided section leaders and pastors and other ministry gifts in the body of Christ.

Remember, the Word of God gives us spiritual authority. Also, your testimony is a powerful tool that the Lord can use to encourage His people in your cell. Your testimony is simply relating what God has done in your life in the past, what He is doing in your life now . . . and what you are believing God is going to do in the future.

Leaders should not give strong advice or correction to a person they do not know very well (unless they are clearly led by the Holy Spirit). Much patience is needed before attempting to correct someone's faults. Simply continue to love and care for them, and many times they will come to you for advice and help. They will see in you an example of how they themselves want to be.

True leaders will take time—all the time that is necessary— to build good, trusting relationships with people. We must build relationships not only within the setting of the home cell meeting, but outside the meeting as well. Through informal time spent in social interaction outside of the meeting context, the time will eventually come when you will feel free to speak into the lives of the people in your cell group because of the trust that has been established. If you don't have a relationship with the people in your cell, it will be very difficult for them to receive advice or correction from you.

Handling the Cell Group's Finances

Many cells in our church take an offering and have a "kitty" that is available for emergencies in the group. (This is not our tithe but an offering for service to others.) The "kitty" is of great help when money is needed quickly. This way the need to collect money from everyone for each emergency is eliminated. Usually the emergency financial need can be met by the home cell group, but if more help is needed, the entire section (small cluster of 2-6 cells) may get involved. It is a good rule of thumb for the cell leader or assistant leader to be the treasurer for the "kitty." Money from this "kitty" is often used by the cell group to purchase flowers for someone who may be in a hospital or recovering from an illness.

In cases where a great deal of money is needed, and it is beyond that which the local cell can handle financially, the cell leader is encouraged to contact the local pastor, the section leader, or someone who is designated to handle this responsibility on the local congregation level. A special "deacon's fund" that is financed by a percentage of the tithes of the church is available to our cell group leaders during times of financial need within the cell, when the need is greater than the cell group can handle alone.

Cell Group Social Activities

Home cell group leaders should periodically initiate activities for their groups to further build relationships. Outings, civic tasks, serving others, eating together and local evangelistic outreaches are just a few examples of the kinds of activities in which a cell group can participate.

People who are gifted in the area of organization may be assigned to help plan activities. It helps to delegate responsibility to others, because it will give people a sense of kinship for what God is doing. Remember, home cell groups are called to be teams, working together to build the kingdom of God in a given area. And please do not forget, our primary focus needs to be prayer and reaching the lost.

It is not necessary for each activity to include everyone in the group. Believers can get together for a baseball game or for a craft session. These are great activities to reach those who do not know Christ.

Cell groups can also meet for breakfast or for a meal during a day off or over a lunch break. Another option is to combine activities for an entire section of cell groups. Before finalizing any plans for a combined event, though, it is best for cell leaders to check with their section leader and local pastor to make sure this event does not conflict with another function of the church of which they are unaware.

Birthdays and Anniversaries

Birthdays and anniversaries are an important part of our lives. Some of the believers that the Lord has placed in your cell group may not have a family who cares about them, or their families may live in another state. Remembering birthdays, anniversaries and other special events with cards, an occasional party, etc., can be a tremendous source of encouragement to them.

Perhaps someone in the cell group could compile a list of birthdays and anniversaries that could be photocopied and passed out to the entire group. As the cell grows and multiplies, this list will be outdated. But the information can still be used as relationships continue even after cell multiplication.

Questions to think about
from Chapter Six

1.   Give the basic job description of a cell leader.

2.   In what ways might a cell leader struggle with "control" in the cell group?

3.   List several ways in which a cell leader is limited in his leadership role.

4.   List some ways a cell leader can give on-the-job training to an assistant leader.

5.   How can a cell leader or assistant cell leader best build a trusting relationship with others in the cell?

CHAPTER 7

LEADING THROUGH SERVANTHOOD

Let this mind be in you which was also in Christ Jesus, who, being in the form of God, did not consider it robbery to be equal with God, but made Himself of no reputation, taking the form of a bondservant . . . (Philippians 2:5-7).

Leadership Means Servanthood

Jesus is our role model for leadership. He was and is the greatest leader who ever lived. He led by being a servant to all of those around Him. He knew who He was because of His intimate relationship with His Father, and out of that relationship He ministered to the needs of individuals.

In the same way, true leaders whom God is using mightily today have these few things in common: they have an intimate relationship with the Father; they know how to pray; they are humble; they are totally dependent on Jesus, and they are servants. If you would observe them when they are not in the spotlight, you would find them serving others.

As a young pastor, I was in Ohio at a leadership meeting and was able to observe a well-known servant of the Lord behind the scenes. He was the kind of person who took every opportunity to notice those around him and was sensitive to their needs. As I watched one day, this man of God led a busboy to the Lord. Then he went out of his way to help this young man find a local church to attend the following weekend. I found this particular leader serving wherever he found an opportunity. His life had a profound impact upon my life. He was a true leader.

Leaders and servants are synonymous in the body of Christ. When DOVE started, we never used the term "leader" in isolation. We called our leaders, "servant-leaders," which implies true leadership, fashioned after Christ, based on serving others.

There is a saying, "Your life is speaking so loudly that I cannot hear the words you are saying." Telling others to serve when we're not serving is like a parent telling a child not to smoke, while puffing on a cigarette. When people see that their leaders do not give in to the self-serving spirit of our age but instead serve and lift each other up, they will be encouraged to do likewise.

There are countless ways we may serve others. We can't serve everyone in the world. We can't meet all the needs; but we are called to a cell group, and we can start there. Set the standard. Be the example. Help someone move, serve a meal, visit a shut-in or pray with someone who has a need. There are hundreds of examples I could give of the servanthood that takes place within cell groups. One cell group I know of gave time and money so a single mom, worn out by the demands of her young children, could take a vacation. Others have given time freely to help remodel or repaint a room in a cell member's house or to repair a car. When a member of a cell group at our church came to a cell meeting one day and announced that her toilet had just broken apart with water gushing everywhere, the cell leader immediately left the meeting to assist the husband in buying and installing a new toilet. When a leader sets the example, soon others will be doing the same, and the body of Christ will experience serving as a life-style.

A servant leader will not rule over people but rather will support them and lift them to God. In the world's system, leaders are expected to dominate those under them, but God has called us to follow the example of His Son, Jesus, and be a servant. By His example, Jesus made it clear that leaders are called to serve.

Jesus Taught His Disciples Servanthood

Jesus called them to Himself and said, "You know that the rulers of the Gentiles lord it over them, and those who are great exercise authority over them. Yet it shall not be so among you; but whoever desires to become great among you let him be your servant. And whoever desires to be first among you, let him be your slave—just as the Son of Man did not come to be served, but to serve, and to give His life a ransom for many" (Matthew 20:25-28).

When the mother of James and John came to Jesus and asked if her sons could sit on the right and left hand of His throne in His kingdom, Jesus told her, "You do not know what you ask." When the other ten disciples heard about it, they were angry, jealous, and resentful. Jesus responded with these words, "Whoever desires to become a leader must become a slave." He did not say that it is wrong to be great, or wrong to be a leader; but greatness according to the world system in which we live is totally different than greatness from Jesus' perspective.

In John 13 we read that Jesus sent His disciples to prepare the Passover. When Jesus arrived, He realized there was a problem. The disciples were arguing about who should wash their feet. Since there was no servant present, and it was customary for a servant to wash the feet of the family and guests as they came in from the dusty streets, the disciples were frustrated.

Without a word, Jesus took a towel and put it around himself. He knelt down and began to wash the disciples' feet. It was too much for Peter to handle. He balked at the idea that Jesus was willing to do the job of a lowly servant. Like Peter, we are sometimes prideful and reluctant to be served. Other times, we must strip away our selfishness in order to serve others. In a home cell group setting, we learn how to serve and to be served.

Leadership Without Servanthood

And they spoke to him, saying, "If you are kind to these people, and please them, and speak good words to them, they will be your servants forever" (II Chronicles 10:7).

Rehoboam became king of Israel after Solomon died. He consulted two groups of counselors for wisdom to govern God's people properly. The older group, who had served before his father, Solomon, spoke the words in the verse above. Then Rehoboam went to the younger group who told him to tell the people, "If you thought you had a heavy yoke to bear under my father, just wait. I will be much tougher!" Listening to the advice of the young men, he lost ten of the twelve tribes of Israel, because he didn't obey the biblical principle of serving.

God says if we serve others and are kind to them, then they will also desire to serve us. Our true motive must be to serve others because Jesus Christ served us unselfishly on the cross two thousand years ago. As we serve out of a pure heart, our sowing in servanthood will allow us to reap the benefits.

Sowing and Reaping Servanthood

An important key to your success as a leader is for you to serve in the home cell group setting in which the Lord has placed you. Ask yourself the question, "How can I best serve this group?"

The greatest training for leadership is to be willing to serve, and then to do whatever needs to be done. Be practical. Find something that needs to be done and do it. Greet people at the door, pick up someone who needs a ride, take a meal, clean someone's home, help a family move, or fix a car.

As a leader, you are an example to those in your group so you need to be setting the standard for servanthood. Like Paul, the apostle, you need to be able to say to those in your home cell group, "Imitate me, just as I also imitate Christ" (I Corinthians 11:1).

As you set the example, others will follow. For instance, when you serve in some capacity at the Sunday morning congregational meetings, such as car parking, ushering, or children's ministry, those in your home group will be challenged to do the same.

Realize that serving others takes time. As a true servant, take all the time that is necessary to serve others in order to build good, trusting relationships. When you spend time with people in social contacts, or do things with others that are just fun or helpful, you are planting the seeds of friendship that will produce a harvest for God's kingdom.

How do you respond to a phone call at 2:00 AM? You need to respond with the heart of a servant! It may take some practice, but a servant will answer, "Hello! What can I do for you?"

Rather than, "Man! Do you know what time it is?" Untimely phone calls can tell us what we are really made of!

If we get upset, we may act like a serpent rising up on the inside to demand our rights as we respond out of a wrong spirit. The serpent in the garden of Eden was only concerned about himself and his "rights." Actually, we don't have any rights because we've laid them down at the foot of the cross. The Lord then gives us privileges and responsibilities.

Jesus gave up His rights as God and went to the cross as a lamb goes to the shearers. As Jesus laid down His rights and gave up His rights as the lamb of God, we must be willing to lay down our lives for others. This does not mean that we are to be wimps who live with a martyr's complex, but it does mean that we can be so secure as children of God that we will gladly lay down our rights and expectations to help others to be strengthened in Christ. See Philippians 2:1-16.

If a neighbor's house is on fire, how do you respond? Do you say, "I hope that big fire truck doesn't drive on my lawn!" or "I hope I don't get smoke in my house"?

No, I'm sure you would say, "I'll do whatever I can to serve my neighbors while they're in this crisis."

If someone in our cell group has a problem, how should we respond? By doing all we can to serve and take care of the problem, not because it's a big hassle for us, and we want to get it over with, but because we want to see this person built strong in Christ. It's not only our actions that are important, but our attitude as well. Lord, teach us to have the heart of a servant.

Hirelings or Shepherds

"I'm sick and tired of people walking all over me." "Everyone is taking advantage of me." "No one appreciates what I'm doing." Those thoughts may cross the mind of every home cell group leader sooner or later because servanthood often requires perseverance, and it's not all fun. But if this becomes our attitude, we'll never make it as a servant leader. Remember, we must give up our rights. We take our selfish rights to the cross of Jesus. Then there will be nothing left to hurt us. Paul said, "I die daily" (I Corinthians 15:31).

If we do not act like servants, the Bible calls us hirelings. A hireling gets paid to tend the sheep, but when the wolves come, the hireling runs away and leaves the sheep defenseless. Hirelings have no personal love for the sheep, no investment of the heart. The Scriptures tell us,

> Now the purpose of the commandment is love from a pure heart, from a good conscience, and from sincere faith . . . (I Timothy 1:5).
> My little children, let us not love in word or in tongue, but in deed and in truth (I John 3:18).

Hireling cell leaders are those tending sheep with the wrong motivation. They are not true shepherds. Their motivation is only for personal gain and personal pride.

There are, of course, times when it is proper to say "no." Jesus left the multitudes and withdrew into the wilderness to pray and be refreshed. At times we must do the same. Our motivation, however, needs to be that the Holy Spirit is leading us to say "no," not because we are just tired of serving.

The Motivation of a Servant Leader

One day, soon after I was married, I decided to surprise my wife and wash the dishes for her while she was out. I scrubbed the dishes spotless and expected a big thanks from LaVerne when she returned. When she didn't even notice, I had to practically gag myself with my dishcloth to keep from prompting her to praise me. I hadn't learned to be a servant. I served for praise, instead of serving because I had the heart of a servant.

The number one motivation of a servant leader is to love God and serve His people out of a heart of love. If our only motivation is to have a good, prosperous, wonderful home cell group—it is wrong. Our first motivation must be to love Jesus, love His people, and desire to reach the lost. When we do that, the natural result will be a good, healthy, exciting home cell group.

Your motivation as a cell leader probably will be tested at times. God may bring people into your life who are hard for you to love. Jesus said,

*. . . in as much as you did it to one of the least of these My
brethren, you did it to Me (Matthew 25:40).*

One night a young man in a backslidden state stopped by
our home. He had been drinking alcohol and vomited all over
himself and the driveway in front of our home. We took him
into our home, loved him and helped him through this situation. God had given us an opportunity to practice the principles of the kingdom of God with proper motivation. Jesus
loved the people He served.

*When He saw the multitudes, He was moved with com-
passion for them, because they were weary and scattered,
like sheep having no shepherd (Matthew 9:36).*

Again, a cell leader's motivation must be that he is moved
with compassion. If we don't feel compassion, we must ask
God to give it to us. Once we have the mind of Christ, we will
eagerly seek those scattered sheep in order to help them.

Sometimes the Lord brings a "brother or sister sandpa-
per" into our lives. Something about them rubs us the wrong
way. The Lord is putting us to the test. If we do not learn the
lesson from our relating to this person, the Lord will probably
bring someone else into our lives who may be even tougher to
handle. Welcome to the real world!

The home cell group setting can give believers the secure
atmosphere they will need to become mature in the body of
Christ. We are being knit together with other people whom
we are learning to love as Jesus does, and our Lord continues
His good work of building His character in us.

Practical Serving Through Hospitality

*Be hospitable to one another without grumbling. As each
one has received a gift, minister it to one another, as good
stewards of the manifold grace of God (I Peter 4:9-10).*

"Hospitality" is cheerfully sharing food, shelter or spiritual refreshment to those God brings into your life. It is using
your home and the material things God has given you as a
means to serve others and build relationships. It is sharing
the love of Jesus in personal and practical ways. And it's fun!

Our homes are centers for ministry. Be open and friendly as you share the things the Lord has given to you. Sitting around the table eating ice cream or playing games usually allows people to feel relaxed, often more so than in a home cell group setting. It is in these types of settings that "pre-Christians" feel most comfortable, because they can see that we are real people.

There is a difference between entertaining and showing hospitality. Entertaining often emphasizes having a nice "party" or meal, while hospitality focuses on the needs of those who have come into our homes. When serving through hospitality, don't hesitate to invite people to your home because of a lack of sumptuous or prepared food. Keep a few snacks or cans of soup on hand just in case; but remember, hospitality doesn't always have to include food!

Keep your home reasonably clean, but don't be anxious about a little dirt or dust. A genuine, warm welcome will bless people a whole lot more than sweeping the floor before they come! We should be much more concerned about fellowship than our home being spotless or having an elaborate meal. Often too much elegance is a hindrance to fellowship. Some of the best times of hospitality are those times when a plate of fruit, hot dogs, ice cream or canned soup is shared as people get to know one another.

Jesus reprimanded Martha, after He came into her home, for being so overwhelmed with all her preparations. She was more concerned about serving than about the One she served. Mary, on the other hand, sought the important thing—fellowship with her guest (Luke 10:38-42).

If God has graced you to serve big meals when people come to your home and you love doing it—that's great. If you become anxious, like Martha, it is a warning light for you to reevaluate. Remember, it's not the food that's important, but the fellowship! The Holy Spirit builds relationships as we spend time with people. We may want to consider setting aside a percentage of our time for hospitality.

Invite Those Who Cannot Invite You Back

Then He also said to him who invited Him, "When you give a dinner or a supper, do not ask your friends, your brothers, your relatives, nor rich neighbors, lest they also invite you back, and you be repaid. But when you give a feast, invite the poor, the maimed, the lame, the blind. And you will be blessed, because they cannot repay you; for you shall be repaid at the resurrection of the just" (Luke 14:12-14).

God is especially honored when we invite those into our homes who cannot invite us back. A young man told a home cell group leader, "The first time I came into your home, I sensed the presence of God." Another told him, "The reason people love to come into your home is because they sense the peace of God." We must realize that the Lord's presence is in our homes. Expect people to sense the presence of the Lord in your home!

Open the door of your home to those who have needs. Romans 12:13 tells us to share with God's people who are in need and to practice hospitality. God is calling us to practical hospitality, expecting nothing in return. It is a commandment, not an option.

Practical Suggestions for Hospitality

When hospitality includes a meal:
- Keep food on hand that can be made quickly.

- If married, the spouse should help prepare and clean up afterward.

- Singles, if your parents or roommates are uncomfortable with your inviting friends to your home when they are present, use your home when they are away, or go to a restaurant.

- Pray with people in your home. A great time to start is before mealtime. (Remember, those who were walking on the road to Emmaus had their spiritual eyes opened as Jesus blessed the food.)

Other suggestions for hospitality:
- Help guests to relax. Give them a drink or a snack so they have something to hold in their hands to keep them from feeling uncomfortable. If they are un-

saved or newly saved and must smoke, be willing to
provide an ashtray.

- Be open to the leading of the Holy Spirit to pray for
  or with them.

- Use tools such as tracts, books, tapes, music, pic-
  tures, and wall plaques to help you in discussing
  spiritual things. The "Two Question Test" booklet [9] is
  an excellent tool to use to lead someone into a
  personal relationship with Jesus.

Serving Through Building Relationships

*. . . from whom the whole body, joined and knit together
by what every joint supplies, according to the effective working by which every part does its share, causes growth of the
body for the edifying of itself in love (Ephesians 4:16).*

We believe that the "joints" the Bible is speaking about
refer to relationships in the body of Christ. Home cell group
meetings are only tools that God uses to build relationships. If
a home cell leader is not a servant, he gets uptight when people
do not come to meetings. If, however, he is a true servant leader,
he will always be building relationships with people outside
of his home cell group meetings; and they will "beat the doors
down" to come to the cell meetings because they know he cares
for them. People recognize sincere servanthood. Children
gather at mealtime around their mother and father because
they are family. They know they are loved and their parents
care for them. They want to be together.

Some potential home cell group leaders have a "preacher's
itch." They are more concerned about speaking to others than
they are in serving others. It is very noble to want to proclaim
the gospel; however, our motivation must be to love people.
We cannot be motivated by selfish gain or recognition. If we
have the heart of a servant, people will come because God
builds His church on loving relationships.

Dwight L. Moody was the Billy Graham of a century ago.
He had twelve hundred young people in his Sunday School
class in Chicago. Many wanted to help him teach. He knew

that only servants would have successful classes so he allowed the young people to go to any class that they wanted. Those teachers who had true servants' hearts and were willing to build relationships with these young people had students in their classes. The others did not. This was Moody's screening process for small group leaders.

Serving Through Encouragement

But exhort one another daily, while it is called "Today," lest any of you be hardened through the deceitfulness of sin (Hebrews 3:13).

Everyone gets discouraged at times. Everyone needs a friend who truly cares, who will listen and be understanding. As a home cell group leader, you may not be able to personally encourage everybody daily. But you can be a catalyst in helping relationships develop. That way everyone in your group will be encouraged regularly.

A catalyst is an outside substance that speeds up a chemical reaction. In fresh, wet concrete, the calcium is the catalyst that causes it to harden quickly.

For example, as new Christians come into your home group, you can pray about which individuals in your home group can properly disciple the new believers. If you sense God telling you that Ross could disciple Tom, a new believer, ask Ross to go along with you and Tom to breakfast or invite both Ross and Tom to your home to see if God would place them together in a relationship. You can be a catalyst in bringing a potential discipleship relationship together, but the Holy Spirit has to do the knitting. You cannot program people. You must pray and encourage and allow God to bring people together. You cannot force relationships to happen.

It is especially important that you encourage a new Christian often. He needs daily contact and encouragement for at least a month after he is saved, and regular contact for six months to a year. He is a spiritual baby and needs his spiritual "diapers" changed. If a new Christian tells you, "I'm discouraged. I don't know if it is worth the hassle of living for the Lord," as a true servant, you will pray with him and encourage him. Then the spiritual baby will say, "I feel much better. Thanks!" It's just a part of helping new Christians grow.

A new tree is very small, weak and spindly when it's first planted, but it grows larger and stronger. When the roots are grounded, it no longer needs a stake to keep the wind from blowing it over. The same principle applies to new Christians. They needs lots of support during their first weeks and months as a Christian.

The greatest ways we can serve the body of Christ is through prayer and giving regular encouragement. Our responsibility is not to hear from God for other people, but rather, we are called to pray for them so that they can hear God's voice for themselves. We train and build them up by holding them up before God's throne in prayer and by modeling for them our dependency on the Word of God. We can be a Godly example to them and share appropriate scriptures with them.

As we care for them and love them, they will soon be built up to hear from God for themselves about decisions that they need to make in their daily lives. The Word of God says,

> But solid food belongs to those who are of full age, that is, those who by reason of use have their senses exercised to discern both good and evil (Hebrews 5:14).

Serving Those Who are
No Longer Active in Our Cell Group

> What man of you, having a hundred sheep, if he loses one of them, does not leave the ninety-nine in the wilderness, and go after the one which is lost until he finds it? (Luke 15:4).

Jesus' first priority was to go after the sheep who left the fold. We need to do the same. When people leave the fellowship that they had with other believers, the enemy is not just sitting nonchalantly in the corner. He is pursuing them.

We are all needy at times. Often when a cell member is depressed or has sinned and is pressed down with guilt, (when he most needs encouragement) he avoids fellow Christians. A cell group needs to be a group of believers that is looking out for one another through the unpredictable turns of life. What should we do when someone is no longer active in the home cell group?

It is important that we do not draw conclusions prematurely. Visit the person or give him a phone call. People know when we sincerely care. Find out why he is not coming to the cell group meetings. Maybe the Lord is calling him to another part of the body of Christ, or maybe he is discouraged. A sheep that is sick needs attention. He may not respond immediately. Give him time for the Spirit of God to work in his life. But don't forget about him or think, "Oh well, he obviously wasn't committed anyway." If he is open to it, pray with him and encourage him to return (unless God is calling him to another place).

Sometimes people do not seem to fit into certain small groups of believers. Perhaps Tammy and Ray soon discover they are not comfortable in the cell they started attending. They seem to have little in common with the others in the cell and have trouble relating. In these cases we encourage Tammy and Ray to visit some other cells until they find their niche. When Tammy and Ray are candid with their cell leader about their struggle to fit in, he can help them find the proper place to be knit in the body of Christ.

A cell leader should never feel insecure when people leave the cell to find another, but rather he should confirm his love and acceptance of the person who struggles to fit in. A cell leader knows that people are like pieces to a puzzle. Some pieces fit together and others do not. When God's people are fit together properly by the Holy Spirit, they will experience the Lord's peace.

During the early days of our church, we discouraged a person from going from one cell group to another cell group, other than when the cell multiplied, because we thought this to be a hindrance to God's people. But, we learned through experience that for the health of the cell, it was more important that each person was assured that the Lord had placed him in the cell he attended.

The Elijah Principle

Elijah the prophet lived out a spiritual principle that the Lord requires cell group leaders, pastors and other Christian leaders to live out in this generation. After suffering from deep depression, Elijah heard his God speak through a still, small voice. The Lord instructed him to recruit Elisha as an "apprentice" and train him to take his place (I Kings 19:11-16). When Elisha asked Elijah for a double portion of his spirit, Elijah gave him clear instructions to receive this "double anointing." After Elijah's departure, Elisha performed twice as many miracles as Elijah!

My prayer for those I am responsible to disciple and train is that they may be used of God in a much greater way than I have been used. Jesus told His disciples that those who believe in Him would do the works He does and even greater works (John 14:12). And John the Baptist, a type of New Testament Elijah, stated clearly, "He must increase, but I must decrease" (John 3:30). John's whole life was consumed with preparing the way for Jesus. The Lord has called us as cell leaders, pastors and Christian leaders to do the same—to see Jesus and others increase as we decrease. This must be our motivation. We are preparing servant leaders for the next generation.

As we disciple others and reach out beyond ourselves, we will see healthy growth in our cell. The next chapter will elaborate on the primary focus every home cell group should have—evangelism and discipleship.

Questions to think about from Chapter Seven

1. What must be the heart motive of true spiritual leaders?

2. What is the difference between "responding" and "reacting"?

3. What is the difference between a servant and a hireling?

4. What do you do when someone continually "rubs you the wrong way"?

5. Give an example of serving through building relationships and serving through encouraging others.

CHAPTER 8

REACHING OUT
BEYOND OURSELVES

And let us consider one another in order to stir up love and good works, not forsaking the assembling of ourselves together, as is the manner of some, but exhorting one another, and so much the more as you see the Day approaching (Hebrews 10:24-25).

The Primary Focus of Meeting in Small Groups

The primary focus of each home cell group should be outreach and discipleship, rather than fellowship, although great fellowship will be a healthy by-product of the home cell group that is constantly reaching out to others.

There will be much prayer and interaction within the group to meet needs and form relationships, but the top priority must always be to bring in the lost. This will cause the cell group to mature and multiply or reproduce another cell. It will give more believers the opportunity to use the gifts the Lord has given to them to reach the lost and make disciples.

We are called to know Him. The greatest catalyst that I know of to grow in Christ is to get our eyes off of ourselves and instead look to Jesus and to the needs of those around us. A group of people who are always looking inward and are content to have the status quo will never grow and multiply. Looking inward prevents growth, like an ingrown toenail, and usually causes pain, competition and stagnation.

When groups are content to stay the same, without knowing it, they build a wall around themselves causing others to feel they are not welcome. The group having a heart to reach

out to others is willing to change, enjoying wonderful fellowship in the process.

When I was newly married and a young missionary, I heard
a man of God quote C.T. Studd, the famous missionary: "I do
not wish to live 'neath sound of church or chapel bell; I want
to run a rescue shop within a yard of hell." These words were
life changing for me.

The main purpose for every cell group must be to run a
rescue shop within a yard of hell. Otherwise, the cell becomes
a social club without any power. The Lord gives us power to
be witnesses, not to sit around and enjoy nice comfortable
"bless-me" meetings.

> *But you shall receive power when the Holy Spirit has come
> upon you; and you shall be witnesses to Me in Jerusalem,
> and in all Judea and Samaria, and to the ends of the earth
> (Acts 1:8).*

The church is not primarily a hospital; it is an army. Although armies do have medical units, they are for the purpose
of getting the soldiers healed so they can get out on the battle-
field and destroy the enemy. The focus is not the medical unit.
The focus is on the battle and in winning the war. We are in a
spiritual war! We do not have time to sit around and play
church like children play war games. We need to rise up in
faith and be the church and destroy the works of darkness in
Jesus' name!

When I was a young man, our nation was in the midst of
the Vietnam war. Every year, Bob Hope would take an entou-
rage to Vietnam to entertain the soldiers. Now let's face the
facts. No one joined the army to go to Vietnam to see Bob Hope.
They went to Vietnam to fight a war! However, while they were
there they had the fringe benefit of being entertained by Bob
Hope and his company.

Although the primary purpose of the cell group is to reach
the lost and disciple new believers, we also experience the
fringe benefit of tremendous fellowship and relationships with
people who care about us. They stand with us as we face hard-
ships and struggles.

I love what Ralph Neighbour, Jr. says in his book, *Where
Do We Go from Here?*

This common vision—reaching the lost and equipping believers for that task—provides the healthy continuity between all the cell groups. It avoids the danger of the common direction being dissipated as different cells use different approaches to their life-styles. There should never, ever, be a 'skunk-works' community of cells, where each one does what is right in the sight of his own eyes. [10]

There will be many different creative approaches to reaching the lost and making disciples as we work together in a small group setting; however, the primary vision must be clear and fixed. We are called to fulfill the Great Commission. We don't necessarily fulfill the Great Commission by having an evangelistic teaching at every cell meeting or think that we must go out on the street to evangelize the lost each week. The main focus of our vision must be to seek the Lord for ways to reach the lost and make disciples.

One cell I was a part of printed up an attractive flyer with a big photo of our smiling cell group. One summer we canvassed the neighborhood where we met as a cell group. We handed out the flyer to those who were newcomers to the community, along with a small house plant welcoming the new families and inviting them to the cell.

Some youth cells have used clowning as a regular outreach ministry for their cell. Dressed as clowns, they go to parks, visit the elderly and generally spread cheer and the gospel wherever they go as they hand out balloons and do short skits.

Picnic evangelism is an informal way to reach family and friends with the message of the gospel. Cell members take the initiative to invite unsaved friends and relatives to a picnic including free food, games and entertainment. Sharing Christ at picnics is a big hit with the DOVE Kenya cell groups in Nairobi; with its warm climate, picnics are possible throughout most of the year. Through the outreach of these family-oriented picnics, relationships are built and people are getting saved.

When cell groups and individuals have evangelism as an integral part of their focus, God often brings nonbelievers right into their cell group settings. Wendy befriended Susi, an atheist East German exchange student at her school. She invited Susi along to her cell group, and over the next several months,

Susi soaked in God's Word and asked many challenging questions of her new-found friends. It was an exciting day for the entire cell group when Susi announced she had made Jesus the Lord of her life and wanted to be baptized.

When individuals in home cell groups challenge each other to reach beyond themselves to make disciples, they will discover that God will give them many creative opportunities. Even if no one immediately comes to Christ through these opportunities, there is a spiritual dynamic released in the cell group that keeps our focus on the harvest fields instead of on ourselves. As we continue to sow, we will eventually reap.

The Oikos Principle

During the early 1980s, a group from our church took a trip to Seoul, Korea, to visit the largest church in the world, Yoido Full Gospel Church. One of the principles that we learned during our time there was the "*oikos* principle."

What is an *oikos*? *Oikos* is the Greek word for household or house of people. Your *oikos* is that group of people whom you relate with on a regular basis. Every believer should apply the *oikos* principle to their lives as a way of infiltrating their spheres of influence with the gospel of Jesus Christ. Acts 10:2 speaks of Cornelius and all of his family (*oikos*),

> *A devout man and one who feared God with all his household, who gave alms generously to the people and prayed to God always.*
> *And the following day they entered Caesarea. Now Cornelius was waiting for them, and had called together his relatives and close friends [his oikos] (Acts 10:24).*

Paul and Silas were in prison. In the midst of an earthquake the jailer became receptive to the gospel. He invited his household to listen to Paul's message and they were all saved. This group of people was his *oikos*.

The *oikos* principle is a strategy of using our existing relationships to evangelize and to make disciples.

Groups of people who are a part of your oikos:

- **Family and relatives.** Your Uncle Jack and Aunt Sadie and cousin Ted are all part of your *oikos*, even if they live far away. If you maintain regular contact with them, they are part of your *oikos*.

- **Those who have common interests with you.** Those who play tennis with you are part of your *oikos*. Anyone you share a common interest with, such as an interest in computers, sewing, playing basketball, playing the guitar—these people are a part of your *oikos*.

- **Those who live in the same geographical location as you.** Your neighbors are a part of your *oikos*.

- **Those who have a common vocation.** Those whom you work with—your fellow employees, are a part of your *oikos*. If you are a construction worker, your *oikos* includes other construction workers. If you are a doctor, other professional people that you would relate with would be included in your *oikos*.

- **Others with whom you have regular contact.** These people may include your dentist, family doctor, mechanic, hairdresser, sales people, school officials, etc.

Those people in your *oikos* group will be much more receptive to the gospel in God's timing because they trust you—you have built a relationship with them.

Sometimes Christians discover they have only other believers in their *oikos*. When this is the case, steps need to be taken to develop new circles of relationships. Some believers join soccer teams, neighborhood organizations and other community groups to increase their *oikos*.

More than twenty years ago, when my wife LaVerne and I and a group of young people began to play baseball, basketball and other sports with youth in our local community, we built relationships with them and they became a part of our *oikos*. Because we established friendships with them on their turf, we could readily share the good news of Jesus. Our *oikos* is part of God's strategy to reach the world.

One day, Jesus ministered to a man who was demon possessed. After he was delivered, the man begged Jesus to follow him. However, Jesus said,

> *Return to your own house, and tell what great things God has done for you. And he went his way and proclaimed throughout the whole city what great things Jesus had done for him" (Luke 8:39).*

Jesus sent him home to his *oikos*!

When Levi invited Jesus to his home for dinner, he invited his *oikos* members (Luke 5:27-32). Zacchaeus had Jesus come to his home, and his whole household was saved. This was his *oikos* (Luke 19:9). Andrew asked Simon to come and get to know Jesus. Simon was Andrew's *oikos* member (John 1:40-42). Philip asked Nathaniel to come and get to know Jesus. Nathaniel was Philip's *oikos* member (John 1:44-45).

Cell members have many everyday *oikos* opportunities. Ryan served as a cell leader in our church until he and his family moved to another state where they are presently involved in cell group ministry. Ryan relates this story from a few years back. He was at the drive-in movies when God used him. "It was just another Saturday night when my wife and I took my young cousin to a Disney movie at the drive-in," said Ryan. "We parked our very used 1971 Toyota with Jesus stickers plastered all over the back window, and I stepped out of the car to go to the snack bar. A guy named Jon stopped me and asked if I was a Christian, and then proceeded to tell me his story of a life lived in sin. I told him how Jesus changed my life and that before I knew God, I was hurting and longing for real purpose. I explained how I had tried to find fulfillment in sports and later had joined the U.S. Marine Corps in hopes that being successful there would bring me a sense of accomplishment. That night, Jon knelt right beside that snack bar at the drive-in and made Jesus the Lord of his life.

"The next week my wife and I, with my little cousin returned to the drive-in and parked the car. This time, before I could even get out of the car, a woman I had never seen before came to the car and asked if I was the person who had prayed with Jon. She asked me to come to her car to meet Jon's mom (notice the expanding *oikos*!). This precious lady, who had been an alcoholic for years, asked Jesus into her life that night and was set free!"

Bob's story is another one that illustrates how an entire family *oikos* was impacted with the gospel. After Bob and his wife found new life and stability in Christ, Bob was burdened for his parents, brothers, and sisters who were far from God. Bob, along with his cell group, prayed that God would allow him to contact his father, with whom the family had lost contact. Although the situation seemed hopeless, through a series of miracles Bob reached his dad, along with other family members on a trip which crisscrossed the U.S. His dad was living with Bob's half sister, and they both received Jesus into their lives. Bob and his sister traveled to another state to share the message of the hope Jesus offers with her brother, and he and his wife were saved. Continuing on to yet another state, Bob contacted his mother, and she responded immediately, "I want to accept Jesus." It helped that Bob's oldest brother had accepted the Lord a few days earlier. Looking back on it, Bob is sure that the Spirit of God moved so freely in response to the many prayers of the believers praying for Bob's "miracle missionary outreach" to his family *oikos*.

The *oikos* strategy is the most natural way of fulfilling the Great Commission. Nearly every Christian has at least 20 people in his or her *oikos*. These 20 people plus their *oikos* gives the potential of 400 contacts (20x20). People want the truth! They are waiting for real Christians whom they can trust to give them the Truth.

You may want to write down your *oikos*. Pray and ask God to show you two or three of the people whom you're most concerned about and begin to pray for these people and reach out to them. If they are unsaved, you will be involved in evangelism. If they are struggling in their Christian lives, God may call you to be involved in discipleship. Either way, you are called to pray for them.

Recently a cell group leader in our church received a phone call from someone in his cell group. "Do you have any holy water?" he was asked. The cell leader did not grow up in a Roman Catholic tradition and was not expecting this type of request; however, he wanted to meet this woman where she was at, so he asked her for further details.

She shared her concern for her daughter and her boyfriend. Strange things were happening in their home. An object had jumped off the stove, and other unexplainable supernatural things were happening in their house. "Could I come over to your daughter and her boyfriend's home to pray?" he asked her.

"Oh yes!" she exclaimed, "and I want to be there when you come." The cell group leader and his wife went over to their home to pray. After a time of sharing the Word of God, this young man received Jesus Christ as Lord. His girlfriend also expressed a desire to obey the Lord, and they were married a short time later. Today they are serving in the cell group and are being discipled and trained to lead others to Jesus.

Another cell group leader shared his faith in Christ with a salesman who came into his place of business. Later the salesman received the Lord and got involved with believers in a cell group in his local area. The cell began to pray for the salesman's unsaved mother. She received the Lord a few weeks before she passed away.

Cell groups who understand the *oikos* principle do not have a hard time focusing their attention on the lost around them. It becomes a very natural way to fulfill the Great Commission.

Called To The Nations

Another way cell groups can reach out beyond themselves is by adopting a missionary or a church leader from a church in another part of the world. We call this "embracing our missionaries."[11] Jesus instructed us to remember that His house is a "house of prayer for all nations" (Mark 11:17). The Lord's heart is in missions. Each cell group needs to have its heart in the same place—in the mission fields of the world.

Cell groups who embrace a missionary send notes of encouragement to the missionary, pray for the missionary, and become a practical link between the missionary and the local church. When the missionary comes home on furlough, the cell group helps to serve the missionary in practical ways: housing, meals, travel, and fellowship.

Some cells adopt a church leader from another nation. Since DOVE Christian Fellowship has a mandate from the Lord to be involved in church planting in the nations of the world, cell members have the opportunity to reach out to believers in other nations who are a part of the same "spiritual family." The Lord has built beautiful relationships between believers in various nations of the world who are involved in these "partner churches."

Each of our international churches in various continents of the world have a vision to multiply and send out laborers to the nations. We believe that new wineskins must be formed in the nations of the world to contain and train new believers during the spiritual awakening that the Lord is sending on the earth! I was so encouraged recently when I spent time with the believers in DOVE Kenya, and heard their vision to reach the nations in the continent of Africa with the good news of Jesus from house to house, city to city, and nation to nation. A few days later I sat with the DOVE Scotland leadership and heard them talk about the vision the Lord has given them to see churches birthed from house to house outside of their nation. And believers in DCF (DOVE Christian Fellowship) New Zealand are already talking and praying about church planting in other nations.

The leadership of these international churches are national leaders whom the Lord has raised up during the past few years. It's a joy to work with these Christian leaders as we labor together in preparing "new wineskins" to preserve the harvest that the Lord is bringing into His kingdom during these last days.

Reaching International Students [12]

One area where cell groups can have a great impact on world missions is in international student ministry. To date, some 500,000 international students study in the United States. This is roughly three-fourths of the entire international student population worldwide. They generally comprise the academic top 5-10% of their young people, and many come from nations closed to traditional Western missionary activity. Furthermore, many universities are now actively recruiting internationals to come and study at their institutions, all the way from top Ivy League Schools to community colleges.

This is a tremendous opportunity for hospitality evangelism. When Paul laid out the qualifications for elders to Titus, he mentioned "hospitality" as one of the required characteristics (Titus 1:8). The Greek word used here for hospitality is *philoxenos*, "to love the foreigner." It is interesting to note that Paul here defines hospitality as that which we do for strangers, not our friends and families.

Through holiday picnics, weekend and semester break housing, recreational activities and invitations to celebrate our religious holidays with us, cell groups can build a circle of friends that can reach the international student with the good news of Jesus Christ. According to surveys, the thing international students who are living in America want most after an American degree is an American friend. Reaching them at this crucial time when they are confronted with relativism and secularism on their campuses can make an impact not only on their own lives, but perhaps even the destiny of a nation.

Since for most internationals, their American degrees will be tickets to positions of relative influence and power in their nations, sharing the gospel with them can have effects that ripple out far beyond their own personal lives. Their contact with Christianity could cause them to look with favor on missions efforts in their own countries and the national churches there. They will most likely have significant influence in their professional sphere and could even receive a call from the Lord to evangelize their own nation in full-time ministry. All it takes is a willingness to give of our time and love, a determination to overcome social and cultural barriers and the boldness to share the gospel with the international student when the time is appropriate.

Homogeneous Cells

According to the New Merriam-Webster Dictionary, *homogeneous* means *of the same or similar kind; of uniform makeup or structure.* In the same way that we have various kinds of living cells in our body, we believe the church should be made up of different kinds of home groups, each having a different target group.

Cells in your body have certain similarities such as a nucleus, but they are all unique and different, depending on the work they do in the body. For example, all liver cells are in the same place—the liver. All heart cells are located in the heart.

Each cell functions in the capacity God created for it for the working of that part.

With home cell groups, each serves the entire church in the way God has ordained in His sovereign wisdom. He places each person where He wants them to be, in order for them to learn and to serve others in a way that is most effective. The most common type of home cells at our church consist of a mixed group with a balance of families, young and older people and singles. These cells may have a mission of intercession, praying actively for people in their communities and the church. Others periodically serve at local rescue missions or serve the homeless. Still others may spend time ministering to lonely senior citizens at the nursing home.

There are a few home cells at our church which have reached out solely to the unchurched children in their communities. They are convinced that today's kids have vast spiritual needs and must be led into an early and deeply meaningful relationship with Jesus Christ before their tender hearts are hardened by the world. The children's cell groups tailor their message for the Nintendo generation of kids. Cells are kept exciting, relevant and create in the children a desire to know God.

Youth cells have been tremendous! Young people who get involved in cell group leadership grow spiritually themselves as they reach out to others. When our daughter Katrina was 15 years old, she began to serve as an assistant cell group leader in a youth cell that met in our home. It gave her the opportunity to grow in the Lord and develop leadership skills that will be with her for her entire life. Many times various youth cells are responsible to plan evangelistic outreaches or social events for the entire youth group in the church or local congregation.

Some cell groups may relate to only businessmen. Their focus is to reach out to other businessmen who need to know Christ. Other groups may have only women, or men, or singles.

One cell at our church was formed by single women who had a burden for unwed mothers. The group initially decorated a box with the word LIFE (Living Instruments for Emmanuel) on it. At each cell meeting, the women would bring small practical gifts for a baby and deposit them in the box. After a few weeks of praying, the Lord led an unwed mother to their group and they spent prime prayer time interceding for her and her unborn child. When the child was born, they had a lot of items to give along with their prayers and encouragement. This cell disbanded soon afterward, but those participating knew they had been called by God for this very special goal of birthing another "living instrument for Emmanuel."

In the same way that we need many kinds of cells in the human body to do the many tasks, so it is in the body of Christ. While each of these home cell groups has its own vision, it needs to flow with the vision of the entire local church (cluster of cells) networking together to fulfill the Great Commission. No cell is an island of its own. It is one part of a larger vision.

We are not just called to be a local church isolated from the rest of the body of Christ. We are called of the Lord to be a part of a movement of the Holy Spirit. We are called to network together in a practical way to build the kingdom of our Lord Jesus Christ in our communities. We are called to extend our hands to others around the world who have "caught the vision" to make disciples in every nation of the world.

Cell Location—By Geography or Relationship?

Every believer should be involved in the particular home cell group that would release him to be fulfilled in Jesus Christ. It may or may not be with people in his local community. The church is built by relationships. Even though most people will find themselves serving alongside believers in their own geographical area, they may initially drive many miles to serve with other believers with whom the Lord has placed them for a particular season of time. If a home cell group is in faith to receive them, people should have the freedom to go to the cell where they believe God has called them, where they feel a unity and oneness or homogeneity with their fellow believers.

Sometime during our early years as a church, we decided to require God's people to get involved in a cell group that was in the closest proximity to where they lived. The principle was right. It is often more effective to be relating to the people within our own geographical area rather than driving miles out of the way to attend a cell group meeting; however, we soon learned that this cannot be dictated. The Holy Spirit is the one who builds people together in relationships. It soon became apparent that some people felt pressured to attend a cell nearby when in reality they had built relationships and felt bonded to others from a more distant cell. Also, this principle didn't work for homogenous cell groups, which drew people with the same basic interests and experiences, but often from diverse geographical areas.

After we realized that we had made a mistake, I confessed this mistake to the cell leaders at a cell leaders' meeting. It released the people to listen to the Holy Spirit and do what He told them to do. As spiritual leaders, we must be sensitive to those we serve. We constantly have the choice between leading by the letter of the law or by the Holy Spirit. Today it is interesting to notice that most people in our church are involved in a cell group in their own area. They are in relationship with these people because they want to be, not because church leadership requires it.

New Believers In The Cell

There are always new people attending various church meetings. Since the cell group is the place for each believer to become actively involved in our church, each new person is encouraged to become immediately involved in a home cell group.

Ralph Neighbour, Jr. says in *Where Do We Go From Here?*

> As the cells grow, many small congregations will be formed. However, they do not replace the cells as the most significant part of church life. For example, no one ever joins a congregation; the only available link to its ministry is to join a cell. [13]

Five times since our inception as a church, we have closed down our Sunday celebration meetings for a period of time. During this time, everyone meets in homes (cell groups) on Sunday mornings. Not only does this strengthen the cell groups in homes (the underground church), but it also does not give an option for believers to be involved in a Sunday morning celebration without becoming involved in the life of the church—the cell church. These have often been rewarding times. Several years ago when the Lord impressed on us to stop meeting in celebrations for one month and instead meet in homes on Sunday mornings, one hundred people were added to the church.

The local pastor may ask a cell group leader to call or visit some of these new people to give them information about their home cell group. If, for some reason, the newcomers do not feel at home in the cell recommended, the cell group leader refers them back to the local pastor who will continue to assist them. We encourage these new people to pray and ask the Lord where He wants them to serve in a home cell group.

Since our church started, we have felt impressed of the Lord to ask for two types of people to be added to His church. The first type (and foremost) is those who are newly saved; the second is those called by the Lord to labor with us in building His church from house to house and reaching the unsaved. In other words, some of the people being directed to our cell may already be Christians who need to be joined to a local church and others may be new converts straight from a life on the streets who may have had little or no church or Bible background.

In the cell group, the more mature Christians can quickly be trained to disciple younger ones in the Lord. This is God's plan for bringing His body to maturity. It's important that everyone is discipled and trained in the basics of the Christian life. We have various materials available to help the cell leader teach the basics of God's Word to new believers in a systematic way. The local pastors have the responsibility to resource the local cell leaders with these "helps." As I mentioned earlier, we are presently writing a series of books for new believers that will introduce them to the basic principles of the Christian life that can be used in a cell group setting. [14]

The Need for Spiritual Fathers

I do not write these things to shame you, but as my beloved children I warn you. For though you might have ten thousand instructors in Christ, yet you do not have many fathers; for in Christ Jesus I have begotten you through the gospel. Therefore I urge you, imitate me. For this reason I have sent Timothy to you, who is my beloved and faithful son in the Lord, who will remind you of my ways in Christ, as I teach everywhere in every church (I Corinthians 4:14-17).

There are many teachers in the church today, but not many fathers. True spiritual fathers (men and women) are sincerely concerned about the welfare of their spiritual children.

We believe that some Christians never really grow to their full potential in God because they never had a spiritual father or mother to invest their life in them. Jesus invested the three years of His earthly ministry in the lives of twelve men. It was the most valuable time He spent on this planet—fathering His spiritual children.

As I travel, I find a desperate need for spiritual fathers. I meet men of God who are used mightily of the Lord in the nations. They have a tremendous anointing as they minister to thousands. But at times when I talk to them in private, they express their need for a spiritual father. I have felt the same need at times in my own life.

New Christians desperately need spiritual fathers. True spiritual leaders are willing to be spiritual fathers to young Christians. One of the pastors who serves a local congregation at DOVE Christian Fellowship in Pennsylvania told me recently that when he received Christ in his mid twenties, a 77 year old man from his local church took him under his wing and discipled him. It made all the difference for this future pastor's spiritual maturity.

All of us are called to be spiritual fathers to someone—maybe a "pre-Christian." Home cell groups are a part of God's plan to establish spiritual fathers for the harvest of new believers who are going to be birthed into the kingdom of God in the coming days.

New parents seldom feel equipped. They learn by doing. It was scary for us when our first child was born. It may be scary for you to take the step of faith to become a spiritual father to someone the Lord brings into your life, but it is a step of obedience that will bring eternal benefits.

Emily, a young girl from our church and only a young Christian herself, started to witness to Debbie, a mother whose children Emily baby-sat. When Debbie, a Jewess, accepted Jesus, Emily took her along to her cell group. Cell members introduced Debbie to Jean, a mature Christian willing to spend extra time with Debbie explaining Scriptures, encouraging her and simply being a friend. When Debbie's parents disowned her for becoming a Christian, Jean and the cell group helped

Debbie through those early difficult months. Over the next year or two, Jean discipled Debbie, rejoicing with her as God brought her victoriously through spiritual and physical crises. Debbie's spiritual journey started when a young Christian took a step of faith and shared Jesus, then God provided a more mature Christian to invest time in Debbie's life to help her along the way.

The Need for New Vessels to Fulfill the Great Commission

A certain woman of the wives of the sons of the prophets cried out to Elisha, saying, "Your servant my husband is dead, and you know that your servant feared the LORD. And the creditor is coming to take my two sons to be his slaves." So Elisha said to her, "What shall I do for you? Tell me, what do you have in the house?" And she said, "Your maidservant has nothing in the house but a jar of oil." Then he said, "Go, borrow vessels from everywhere, from all your neighbors—empty vessels; do not gather just a few. And when you have come in, you shall shut the door behind you and your sons; then pour it into all those vessels, and set aside the full ones." So she went from him and shut the door behind her and her sons, who brought the vessels to her; and she poured it out. Now it came to pass, when the vessels were full, that she said to her son, "Bring me another vessel." And he said to her, "There is not another vessel." So the oil ceased. Then she came and told the man of God. And he said, "Go, sell the oil and pay your debt; and you and your sons live on the rest" (II Kings 4:1-7).

Notice that the oil stopped when the vessels (containers) were filled. The Lord promises to pour out His Holy Spirit in these last days. Flexible containers must be prepared for the great harvest that is on the horizon. Is it possible that the Lord is waiting for His church to prepare the proper containers so He can pour out His Spirit?

I mentioned earlier that during the Jesus movement in the 1970s thousands were saved, but many were lost. There were not enough "new containers" willing to be flexible enough to embrace these new believers. The Lord is waiting for us to prepare new vessels before He will pour out the oil of His revival. Each of these vessels has a spout on it so that it can pour out the oil of God's blessing through His people into other vessels.

Now is the time to prepare leadership for the coming awakening (harvest). We cannot force new Christians into our meetings—we must prepare new vessels for the new oil. Forming new vessels will enhance the Lord's commission to make disciples. Many new types of vessels (cell groups and local congregations) must be formed. Let's get about our Father's business.

Discipleship In Its Truest Sense

Go therefore and make disciples of all the nations, baptizing them in the name of the Father and of the Son and of the Holy Spirit, teaching them to observe all things that I have commanded you; and lo, I am with you always, even to the end of the age (Matthew 28:19-20).

Making disciples is the charge that has been given to every believer in the Lord Jesus Christ. Christians call it "The Great Commission." This commission from our Lord Jesus is not an option. We are called to make disciples.

Discipleship in its truest sense is not something to be afraid of. It simply means being a friend to someone and helping them grow in their relationship with God. When Beth, a single mom, joined Cathy's cell group, Cathy at first felt led to pray for Beth and her daughter every day. Cathy and Beth were as different as night and day and seemed to have little in common, but they soon realized that God was bonding them together in a precious way. Cathy became a support system for Beth in her early Christian days. Today, Beth, beautifully matured in Jesus, is often an encouragement to Cathy.

A cell leader who only wants to teach or lead, but not be involved in making disciples would not be successful in helping people come to maturity in Christ. Sheep need shepherds, someone who will not only tell them which way to go, but will walk side by side with them, even helping them to carry their load if necessary. Our focus must be on Jesus and helping others become conformed into the image of Christ, not fulfilling our gifts. The Lord will give us grace to fulfill His calling in our lives and use the giftings in our lives as we maintain His priorities.

God has called us to use the home cell groups as new vessels for the harvest. They are tools for making disciples, beginning in our local area and then reaching out to the nations. Every ministry in our church assists in the building of these "underground churches"—the home cell groups. For example, the purpose for the mission department is to help every believer in every cell group experience the blessing of teaming with others to reach the nations. The counseling department is a service department, helping each believer to be equipped to help others as Jesus builds His church from house to house, city to city, and nation to nation.

An exciting, modern day example of an underground church experiencing a great revival and making many new disciples took place in Ethiopia. In 1982 half of all the evangelical churches in Ethiopia were closed due to harassment, legal banning, and persecution. The Meserete Kristos Church fell under a complete ban. All of their church buildings were seized and used for other purposes. Several of their prominent leaders were imprisoned for years without trial or accusation.

The church membership at that time was approximately 5000 believers. The fires of persecution got hotter and hotter each year forcing them to go underground and meet in clandestine home groups. Nearly a decade later the Marxist government fell. The same government leaders who closed the doors of the church buildings a few years before, led the procession of God's people back into the buildings. However, the church had grown "underground" from 5000 to over 50,000 people!

During persecution, these believers met from house to house in small groups. Hundreds of believers began to get involved in the work of ministry in these cell groups. They no longer were focusing on the church building or the programs of the church. Their time together was spent in prayer, reaching the lost, and making disciples.

In my study of church history, over and over again before any great move of the Holy Spirit, there were small groups of dedicated people who prayed and searched the Scriptures. The great revivals and outpourings of the Holy Spirit are usually traced to these seemingly insignificant gatherings of a few fervent intercessors.

Is it going to take persecution for us to experience this same kind of revival? Focusing on Jesus and the church meeting from house to house takes our emphasis off of meetings and programs. We can focus on Jesus and on the Great Commission. Is it possible that sometimes we are so busy going to church meetings that we do not have time to be Christians? Cell groups provide the atmosphere for believers to learn practical Christian living as they reach out and make disciples. The next chapter offers some practical and specific ideas how a cell meeting may be conducted.

Questions to think about
from Chapter Eight

1. Explain how "outreach" is the primary focus of a cell group.

2. If a cell is actively engaged in winning lost souls, what "fringe benefits" can they expect to enjoy?

3. Make a list of persons that you presently have in your *oikos*.

4. If you are currently involved in a cell group, how often does your cell have unsaved people as a part of it?

5. What is a spiritual father? Do you have a spiritual father? Are you a spiritual father to another person?

CHAPTER 9

THE HOME GROUP MEETINGS

The dynamics of a cell meeting are completely different from a celebration meeting. Cell groups are small groups of believers meeting together where everyone has the opportunity to share life experiences and to be open with the others in the cell group. Since the cell group only has a small group of people, there are not as many spiritual gifts available as there are in a larger celebration meeting.

For example, there may not be anyone in the cell gifted as a worship leader, yet at the celebration there may be many worship leaders. So then, the purpose of the cell meeting is not to try to be a miniature celebration meeting, but instead to be a safe environment for the Lord's people to share their lives together, pray, share the Word of God and receive a vision from the Lord to reach the lost.

We do not come together to receive "deep teaching" in the cell group setting. In-depth teaching can be received at celebration meetings (where there is a focus on teaching God's Word), at training events, through reading books and listening to teaching tapes. Members of our cell groups have received further training by signing up to take Bible courses at a School of the Bible we have offered in sessions throughout the year, including Biblical teaching on marriage, personal finances, teachings applicable to youth, training children, prayer, operating in the gifts of the Spirit, evangelism, etc.

In a cell group setting we really need to learn about "practical Christian living." In cell groups we grow in spiritual maturity because we learn to accept and love our brothers and sisters unconditionally. It's a place where we pray for each other's brokenness as we witness the healing work of Jesus. Compassion surrounds us and encouragement lightens our loads. When we hear what God is teaching others in their personal lives, it teaches us. The home cell group setting becomes a workshop where we learn about serving, accountability, prayer and worship. It is where we can be brought as believers to a place of strength and maturity. We learn about practical Christian living as we watch over one another, knowing that as we serve, we are all growing stronger in Christ.

Teaching in the Cell Group

A teaching presented during the cell meeting should be short with comments and response for practical application. We recommend that these messages last about ten to fifteen minutes.

Since it could become a burden for many cell leaders to study and prepare a new cell teaching for each meeting, we provide cassette tapes containing a Bible teaching, along with a set of notes for the cell leader, well in advance of the meetings. The cell leader then is responsible to get the teaching for the meeting into his own spirit first, as preparation, before teaching it. This resource allows the cell group leader, who is probably working a full-time job, to put more time into prayer and practical discipleship.

This prepared teaching is not a requirement to teach, but an option as each cell leader prays about what the Lord wants the cell group to do together each week. The cell leaders are encouraged, however, to study the teaching that is prepared as personal training and development for them as cell group leaders even if they don't use it to teach. Our church has hundreds of cell group teachings available with many subjects which cell leaders can obtain from their local pastors or from our corporate resource center. Remember that every cell group is at a different place spiritually. If the people in the cell are largely new believers, the teachings should be much different compared to a cell group that has all mature believers who need to be motivated and stirred to win the lost.

For many years when our church was smaller, we encouraged all cell groups to use the same teaching week by week. However, as the church grew, we discovered that the needs in the various cell groups became much more diverse. There are still occasions when the Lord may be giving a specific word for the whole church at the same time. On the other hand, the more we can remain flexible to obey the Holy Spirit in our cell group meetings, the more fruitful our cell groups will become.

Those who teach are encouraged to use modern day parables, stories that apply to the lives of God's people. Jesus constantly taught with stories. The people remembered the story, and then they remembered the spiritual truth. A key to teaching is to be a good story teller. Some years ago I developed an interest in Dwight L. Moody, the famous evangelist of the nineteenth century. I remember my amazement when I picked up a book of his sermons. They were filled with stories. John Wesley used to rehearse his sermons in the presence of his nine year old servant girl. If she could understand it, then he would give the message publicly.

Again, I want to emphasize that each group is encouraged to do whatever is most effective for their cell group to be reaching the lost and making disciples. If someone needs healing in the group or has a friend who is sick, perhaps there should be a short teaching on healing with a time of prayer for the sick.

Some cell groups play the cassette tape of the teaching which has been provided for them. Then they take their Bibles and discuss the truths that were taught and help one another apply them to their own personal lives.

At times we have also prepared video tapes to be used on the cell group level for the purpose of teaching. A prominent Bible teacher was with us a few years ago, and we felt that the messages that he taught were important enough for us to mass produce on video tape. These teachings were then given by video in each of the cell groups for about a two month period.

Some cell groups have used our church's Biblical Foundation Course as a teaching format for a season. Others have used other printed materials.

Another refreshing thing that can happen is to invite an apostle, a prophet, an evangelist, a pastor or a teacher into your cell group to minister to God's people. These "circuit riders" can impart more under the anointing of the Holy Spirit in one evening than you could imagine. The question to ask is: What will be the most effective thing for our cell group to do for every person to know Jesus in an intimate way and fulfill the Great Commission?

Choosing a Home for the Meeting Place

When deciding whose home your group will meet in, the following are some things to consider. Is the location central for the majority of the people in your group? Does it have a large enough room for the group to gather in with space for newcomers? If needed, is there a separate room for children's ministry? Does the home offer a comfortable and relaxing atmosphere to adults and children as well? Are the hosts financially able to meet the needs that hosting a group involves? This question is of special significance in cultures where serving coffee, tea, and cookies or biscuits is expected.

In the past, many times the cells of our church met in the same home until the group multiplied or the location was no longer suitable. More recently, many of the cells have found it much more advantageous for the cell group to rotate to various homes of the cell members. Those who are willing to host the meeting find that it is a special blessing to have the church meet in their home!

I like what Ralph Neighbour, Jr. says about meeting from house to house, in *Where Do We Go From Here?*

> When the cell meets at the same house all the time, several major setbacks occur. The first is the miserable task of the poor housewife to get her place cleaned up for company every Tuesday night. After a while, that gets old!
>
> The second setback is that the group quickly establishes that this is "Bill and Margie's group." Mutual ownership is destroyed. Accountability for the gatherings is watered down.
>
> The third setback is that people never get to really know each other until they spend time in all the homes in the group.[15]

Meeting Time and Format

In the past at our church, most cell groups have met twice a month and then they were encouraged to meet together to pray during the "off week." Recently, many cells have found it more effective to meet together each week. Sometimes groups will alternate a regular meeting with an outreach or game night.

Or sometimes the women will meet separately from the men on the off weeks. The men or women may get together for breakfast or go bowling.

Since the cell meeting and relationships are a priority in the church, believers should be spending at least as much time in some type of a cell group context, as in other types of church meetings. We are not minimizing the effectiveness of meetings of congregations or larger corporate celebrations. They are also important. The New Testament church met in public meetings and from house to house (Acts 20:20). The pressure of the church in today's society will quickly try to squeeze us into a mold that has been set in tradition for the past 1700 years. This mold has the focus of the church as meeting within the four walls of a building every Sunday morning, Sunday evening and Wednesday night.

It is important that you follow the leading of the Holy Spirit when you conduct your cell group meetings. Unless you are clearly led otherwise, I encourage you to keep the meeting to about one to one and a half hours. Another helpful hint is to always be prepared! Have a schedule and stick to it, unless you know that the Holy Spirit is leading otherwise. Always be open to the leading of the Holy Spirit.

There is no excuse to say you are "following the Holy Spirit" if in actuality you are simply unprepared. Many times we say we are following the Holy Spirit when in reality we have been lazy and undisciplined. This is a disgrace to our Lord and to His people. To waste people's time shows poor leadership.

Prayer should be planned as a vital part of your time together. Ask someone beforehand to open with prayer. Have a time for intercession and praise. Give everyone an opportunity to pray. Be helpful and encouraging when people are learning to pray out loud.

One of the men in a cell group that I led a few years back was scared to pray publicly. He knew that he had to deal with this fear. He told me to ask him to pray in front of the other men in the cell group when we met together to pray every other week before work in the mornings. As I asked him to pray and encouraged him, he went on to lead various cell groups in the years that followed. He just needed some encouragement and accountability in the cell group setting.

Teach people to pray. Encourage short conversational prayers. Explain the importance of praying in agreement according to Matthew 18:19-20,

> Again I say to you that if two of you agree on earth concerning anything that they ask, it will be done for them by My Father in heaven. For where two or three are gathered together in My name, I am there in the midst of them.

I am really hesitant to give guidelines for what should happen at a cell meeting because I believe it is so easy to trust the format rather than being truly open to what the Holy Spirit wants you to do. But so many pastors and cell group leaders have asked me to share these guidelines that I believe I need to address this subject.

Many times cell group meetings include a time of worship, testimonies, a short teaching (approximately 10-15 minutes), a time for response to the teaching, announcements, prayer, and sharing of life together. The format can be changed and altered in a thousand ways. You do not have to do all of these things, or in reality you do not need to do any of these things. Every time you come together should be different. Do not get stuck in a rut. I once heard that a rut is a grave with the ends knocked out. Doing the same thing week after week will bring spiritual death into your cell group.

Remember your mission—to pray, reach the lost, and make disciples. Unless we keep our eyes firmly fixed on our mission, we will forget why we are getting together. The enemy will deceive us and put us asleep spiritually while the world goes to hell around us.

Make sure you start and stop your meetings on the agreed times, unless the Holy Spirit leads you otherwise. Be respectful of other people's time, especially parents of little babies and school children who must study.

The time following the meeting is full of opportunities for sharing and meeting the spiritual needs of the people. This is often the most important time of the cell meeting. Those who must leave may go, and those who want to seek help from the cell leader or others in the cell group are free to do so. Many times after cell group meetings, small clusters of people may gather together in various areas of the home to share heart to heart and pray together. These times of informal fellowship are invaluable as our fellow believers surround us with compassion and give us the courage to keep going so we will be able to stand tall, embodying the very fullness of Christ (Ephesians 4:11-16).

Maintaining Order During the Meeting

Keep the meeting moving and alive. Whoever has been given responsibility for a particular part of the meeting must be enthusiastic about his part, or the meeting will falter and be of no benefit. People will be bored.

If there are those who constantly interrupt, they should be gently confronted with the truth that they need to "consider others as more important than themselves." I Corinthians 14:26 tells us,

> *What then shall we say, brothers? When you come together, everyone has a hymn, or a word of instruction, a revelation, a tongue or an interpretation. All of these must be done for the strengthening of the church (NIV).*

Nothing should be permitted to take place that does not line up with the Scriptures or quenches the Holy Spirit. For example, one evening I was leading a cell meeting when one of the men began to "pray" in a tongue that sent chills up my spine. There was something drastically wrong. I turned the meeting over to someone else and along with another Christian brother took this man into another room to minister to him. It became apparent that he needed deliverance and the voice he was "praying" in was the voice of a demon.

If you feel that your meetings are getting out of hand because one person monopolizes the time, you may need to encourage that person who is overly verbal to allow others time to share. Ask him to stick to a time limit.

If someone takes the meeting "down a side street" by getting off the subject, you can tactfully tell him that you will be happy to talk to him privately about it after the meeting. This way you can honor him as a person, and you can keep the meeting from becoming boring for the rest of the people.

Gifts of the Spirit in the Cell Group Meetings

Each person in the home cell group should be learning how to be sensitive to the Holy Spirit's promptings. For example, the cell leader should encourage each person to contribute to the supernatural life of the group. A close-knit cell group will provide an ideal setting to step out and begin exercising the gifts of the Spirit. As God directs, the cell leader needs to be sensitive and remember that it is a bit scary to give a prophecy or a word of knowledge for the first time.

The first time that I ever prophesied was in a group of three people. I was so scared, my palms were sweaty, but at the encouragement of my two brothers in Christ I took a step of faith and prophesied for the first time.

Often the Holy Spirit will activate gifts in people during a time of worship or prayer, but opportunity must be given for the Holy Spirit to do His work. Invite Him to come among you and give Him liberty to operate in the group.

The Holy Spirit may give one person a prophecy. He may give another a word of wisdom or a word of knowledge (I Corinthians 12:8). He may call you to take some time for gifts of healing or the working of miracles to flow.

The gifts of the Holy Spirit have been given to us to edify the church, to minister to the unsaved, and to confound the unbelieving (I Corinthians 14). The cell group is the place for training and releasing the gifts of the Holy Spirit so that these gifts become a part of our everyday lives as we reach out in faith to pray for miracles for people in a hurting world.

As a cell group leader, you may sense a "stirring in your heart." Don't be afraid to express this to the others in the cell group. Sometimes that's all the encouragement needed in order for someone to step out in faith. Cell members may give words of wisdom and knowledge to others in the cell, and healing will flow.

If the Holy Spirit tells you to have a time of kneeling and prayer, that is exactly what you should do. A deep prayer session may be the most moving and exciting thing your group may ever experience. To allow God to move will truly be the best thing your cell can do. Always be sensitive to new people in the group. Explain to them in private from the Scriptures why you do certain things.

All in all, the home cell group is a gathering God is using in the Christian's school of the Holy Spirit. Personal prophecies can be given with the understanding that "we prophesy in part" and that there are proper ways to process that type of a word from the Lord.

Sometimes it is wise if personal prophecies can be recorded or written down to be given to the local church leadership or pastor for confirmation. The Bible tells us to "test all things" and "do all things properly and in an orderly manner." It is best that personal prophecies not be given "outside" or in a corner somewhere without someone in leadership present. This will insure proper spiritual protection to the person giving the personal prophecy as well as to the person receiving it. It will also help alleviate anyone being misled or improperly responding to the prophetic word that they have received.

If a cell group has a lack of experience in the gifts of the Holy Spirit, my suggestion would be to invite someone into the cell who has a prophetic gift to equip the believers in this area. After a few weeks of equipping by a prophetic minister, the people in the group will find a new freedom to operate in the gifts of the Holy Spirit.

Call People By Their Name

In America, it is important that you know the people in your group on a first name basis. Other nations and cultures may require us to use proper names or family names. Americans, however, usually address people by their first name as a common courtesy. It also draws them out and encourages them to participate. When teaching the Word of God, use the names of the people in the cell as often as possible when you give illustrations or parables. It makes people feel important, and they should, because God thinks they are!

Jesus, the Good Shepherd, knows each of His sheep and calls them by name. As the cell group leader spends time in prayer for each person in his group on a daily basis, he will find it will not take long until he knows each name by heart.

In case you have real difficulty remembering names, here is a helpful tip: When meeting someone and hearing his name for the first time, think of someone else you know who has the same name. It could be the name of a friend or family member or a character in the Bible. Then remember that name every time you think of the new person until you have it memorized.

Don't Put People "On The Spot"

Try to get everyone to participate in the cell meeting; however, it is important that you do not embarrass anyone by having them read Scripture, or pray, or explain a verse if they are uncomfortable with this. Some people in the cell group you may know well enough to be certain that they would not object. If you are not sure, you should ask them prior to the meeting. Give them the freedom to decline if they need to.

I have a friend who was "put on the spot" in a Sunday School class as the class members were reading the Scriptures one person at a time. My friend had difficulty reading and was so uncomfortable and embarrassed that it took twenty years to get enough courage to go back to a Sunday School class. A sensitive leader could have saved my friend a lot of pain.

Ask Johnny if he is willing and ready to give a public testimony before telling the group he has something to share. Encourage timid Christians to be open, but speak with them privately about it first.

These introverted or shy people are best reached by gaining their confidence after the meeting. If there is someone who sits in the corner and hesitates to join in, make a point of spending time with him in casual conversation a few times and gradually enlist him to take part in the meeting and activities. Remember how you felt when you were a new Christian.

Worship Leaders

If possible, each cell group should try to have at least one person designated to lead the group in worship. If a person is selected for this ministry, he does not need to play an instrument—although many do—but should be able to lead in worshipful singing unto the Lord.

Some cell groups do not have a worship leader and spend time in prayer instead. Others make use of recorded tapes and sound tracks that enhance the times of singing unto the Lord. Cell members can be encouraged to come to the cell group meetings with a song or a hymn to share with the cell. When everyone feels a sense of responsibility before the Lord for what happens at the cell group meeting, you can expect the Lord to move through His body in a powerful way.

The worship leader should stick to the allotted time given by the cell leader for the worship period. He also should have song sheets available for new members who would be uncomfortable worshipping without knowing the words.

Let me emphasize again, the cell meeting is not a mini-celebration meeting. To compare the cell to a celebration meeting of hundreds or thousands would be very unprofitable.

Ministering To The Children

Many times cell groups that have families with children provide ministry time for the older children or nursery for the younger ones. You could either have a regular leader for the children or have different people in the group take turns. Sometimes people from one cell will serve the children in another cell if the two groups meet at different times. Whatever you do, do not place the children in front of the television set as a baby-sitter; however, the use of Christian videos with a responsible teacher is appropriate as a part of the ministry to children.

We think it is best for two people to minister together to the children. In a day when child abuse has reached the proportions that it has (statistics now tell us that one out of every three girls and one in seven boys will be sexually assaulted before they reach the age of 18), two ministering together for the purpose of accountability is advisable.

Some cell groups gear the entire cell group meeting to minister to the families as a whole because they find this format the most advantageous for their cell group. The children are part of the worship, prayer, sharing and ministry. We must listen to the Holy Spirit for His direction on these matters. What is right for one cell group may not be right for another.

Often the children are included in the worship time before being dismissed to their own group for the remainder of the meeting. In other cells, the children are a part of the entire cell meeting. Each cell group has its own personality and relates to a certain group of people, so many do it differently.

When our daughter Charita was twelve, she felt a special call to serve the younger children in our cell group. She used her organizational and teaching gifts to gather materials together suitable for Bible stories. She planned craft activities and collected prizes to give to the children when they learned their Bible verses, as well as planned skits, puppet shows, and games. The kids loved it and looked forward to coming to the cell group because they felt included and cared for.

Some home cell groups have a special youth night or children's night. On these nights the youth in the home cell group plan the entire meeting. Other times the children may give a special program. Be creative.

Snacks And Food

Having snacks or food during fellowship can be a real blessing, but care must be taken that it does not become competitive or a burden to anyone. Some cells only serve snacks on special occasions, such as birthday parties or other celebrations. In some cases, having snacks at the conclusion of each cell meeting could be distracting to what the Holy Spirit is doing. Be sensitive to the leading of the Holy Spirit and clearly communicate to everyone what you believe the Lord is saying about this. If you meet in various homes week to week, the person or family that is opening their home may feel pressure to do something that someone else has done, but may not have the time or the finances. This could cause unnecessary tension.

Be Flexible And Creative

To keep the meetings vibrant, don't settle into a dull routine. Plan well ahead for new activities. Talk with other home cell groups to find out what they are doing. Ask the people in your group periodically for suggestions. Resource books such as *Home Fellowship Meetings, Creative Ideas,* by Don and Gail Gunstone and the *Shepherd's Guidebook* by Ralph Neighbour Jr. can be tremendous resources. [16]

On occasion, when someone in the group is in need, go to their home to help them instead of having the regular cell meeting. One night our cell group met, and we realized that the one couple was missing because they had fallen behind on their yard work. Rather than condemning them for missing the cell meeting, we laid aside our plans for the meeting and went to their home and helped them. It was a tremendous time ministering to them in a practical way.

Other times we have joined another cell (or the whole section) for an evening together. These kinds of alternatives help keep the group flexible.

Water Baptism

Then Peter said to them, "Repent, and let every one of you be baptized in the name of Jesus Christ for the remission of sins; and you shall receive the gift of the Holy Spirit" (Acts 2:38).

God's will is for new believers to be added to the church daily! When a new believer comes into a home cell group, the cell leader should inquire if he was baptized in water. If he has not been, the cell group leader or another believer in the cell group can serve that person by baptizing him. The section leader or local pastor is available to give training in this area. They also can help the cell group leader with the details of locating a proper place for the baptism. We have used swimming pools, bathtubs, rivers . . . anywhere where there was water available for a baptism. Take this opportunity to teach new believers the purpose of water baptism from the Scriptures.

Water baptism signifies our "death" in Christ and our "resurrection" with Him into new life as we come out of the water. Have a time of prayer for the person. Many times words of prophecy will be given at this time.

Often the entire home cell group and the person's family will be in attendance which provides a good opportunity for witnessing and celebrating. Sometimes the new convert will give his or her testimony during the baptism. Romans 6:1-10 provides a great text from which to share the gospel at the water baptism site.

Communion, Love Feasts

Each cell has the liberty to celebrate the Lord's Supper as often as it wishes in the home group setting. It is a vital part of the Christian life to remember and meditate on the death and resurrection of our Lord Jesus Christ. Paul stressed it was the most important issue he could preach—" . . . Jesus Christ, and Him crucified" (I Corinthians 2:2).

It is important that the Holy Communion time be kept reverent with a sense of celebration as the Holy Spirit leads. The leader should read or discuss passages such as I Corinthians 11:23-26, or passages on the Last Supper from the gospels, about the death and resurrection of Jesus. Sometimes it can be very meaningful to have someone in the home cell group sing a special song, or background music could be played to encourage the people as they share communion together.

Some of the cell groups in our church have had a meaningful and spiritual time of washing each other's feet as a symbol of servanthood, or some have had a love feast (a meal together) as found in John, chapter 13. Care must be given to properly explain and adequately prepare for such special times, but the outcome can be a tremendous blessing for each member of the group.

Baby Dedication

For this child I prayed, and the Lord has granted me my petition which I asked of Him. Therefore I also have lent him to the Lord; as long as he lives he shall be lent to the Lord (I Samuel 1:27-28).

When a newborn is dedicated to the Lord, it is a special time for the entire group as well as for relatives of the child who may not be a part of the home cell group or the church. It can be a time of joy and a powerful witness. The group should affirm their willingness to help the parents in training the child for the glory of God.

Sometimes the cell leader will read the story of baby Jesus' dedication found in Luke chapter two, and allow the parents to express their commitment to bring up the child in the nurture and admonition of the Lord.

The cell leader should communicate with the local pastor regarding the new baby's dedication to the Lord in the cell group setting. Sometimes baby dedications are handled at the congregational level and other times at the cell level. Sometimes both are done.

The Multiplication Process

The process of cell multiplication in human cells is called "mitosis." It is multiplication by dividing. One cell becomes two, and each continues to grow until they, too, divide and separate to become four cells, etc. Each home cell group goes through a period of gestation (growth and learning) before it can give birth to a new group.

For a new home cell group, the first few months is a good time for sharing testimonies and building new relationships. Everyone could share how they were brought to the Lord, how they were baptized in the Holy Spirit, how they came to this local church, etc. It is very healthy to share these spiritual experiences. It is in this way that people begin to be knit together and understand more about each other. It also provides opportunities for deeper friendships to develop.

During the next few months there should be more of an emphasis on bringing others into the cell group. Share with friends, neighbors, those at work, and loved ones about Jesus and how He has changed your life. Tell them what is going on—what God is doing in your group. Expect people to come to a place of faith in Jesus Christ.

The cell group leader needs to continue to give a clear vision to the cell that it will multiply into two cells. Then, as the group gets larger, the people will begin to talk about birthing a new cell. I was a member of one home cell group that became large and cumbersome. We decided to meet in smaller groups for prayer during our cell meetings. A month or two later we decided to take these four prayer groups and meet in separate homes. We were still a part of the same large group, but we met at times as smaller prayer meetings in different homes instead of always attending the regular cell group meeting as often as we had before. After doing this for awhile, some of the small prayer groups became so excited about their small group, that they decided to begin a new home cell group. It is said that some people never learn to swim until they jump into the water! The same is true with cell multiplication.

Consequently, there should be a lot of prayer and open communication about specific upcoming changes. Give the people some time to get used to the new idea until it is birthed in their own hearts and they welcome it. Then it will not be a traumatic thing, but something that everyone will look forward to with enthusiasm and faith. Encourage each person to seek the Lord's wisdom on any proposed change and get back to you with a response. It is best if the move can be confirmed by as many people as possible in the group. During this time the cell leaders should be accountable to the local church leaders who will pray with them and assist them in any way possible.

Remember, growth is healthy. A healthy church is a growing church—numerically, by the adding of people to His kingdom and in maturity, by growing closer to our Lord Jesus.

"How often should a cell group multiply?" is one of the questions that I am most often asked by pastors and cell group leaders. The answer depends upon what the Holy Spirit is saying to you and in which culture you are living.

In our culture, we believe that believers in every cell group should ask the Lord for the grace to spawn a new group each year. Other cultures and nations could be much more often. Encouraging each cell group to multiply each year is a goal to encourage; however, we do not make it a requirement. Many cells will have the grace to multiply more often than once a year.

Goals are important, but they must be birthed by the Holy Spirit and attainable. We must admit, some of the goals that we set in our early years as a church are embarrassing. We set a goal early on to be a church of 40,000 people during the first years we were in existence. In retrospect, this goal was based much more on a mathematical calculation than it was on a word from the Holy Spirit!

Another time, after a group from our church returned from our first trip to visit the world's largest church in Seoul, Korea, we were all excited about quickly setting goals. Although the concept of goal setting was good and needed, we set goals that were not spiritually attainable for all of the cell group leaders. We told all cell group leaders that they needed to multiply their cell groups every six months. This is certainly a good goal; however, each cell group and leader is at a different place spiritually. Although some cell groups enthusiastically trusted the Lord for their cell group to multiply every six months, other cell leaders began to "burn out" because of not being able to meet these expectations. Along with our leadership team, I asked their forgiveness for placing these stringent requirements on them.

We do believe, however, that to trust the Lord for at least two people or families to come to Christ through our cell group each year is certainly not setting a goal that is too high. Those who have no spirit-led goals often have no vision. And without a clear vision, the Scriptures tell us we will perish.

When it is time for a cell to multiply, everyone will be ready for it because they were preparing for this process all along. Often a cell group has been praying for a particular town or area, and a few cell members who live there subsequently feel called to begin a new cell in that town. Because assistant leaders have been raised up previously in the cell, there is always ongoing leadership potential to accommodate multiplication.

And remember, the purpose for multiplication in the cell group is to see God's people released to train others and fulfill God's Word (II Timothy 2:2), not just to meet a goal. The early believers walked in the fear of the Lord and in the comfort of the Holy Spirit and were multiplied (Acts 9:31). We are called to do the same.

Recently a cell group that was multiplying invited all of the other cells in their city to celebrate the cell group multiplication at a local restaurant. Nearly everyone came from the cell groups in the entire city. It was a festive occasion. There was a time of rejoicing that the Lord had given the cell group the opportunity to multiply into two cells. There was a time of prayer for the new and original cell group leaders. Since the multiplication took place, the new cell group has doubled in size and the original cell is nearly as large as it was a few months ago.

The natural tendency is for believers in the cell groups to want to stay together. However, if we can understand our Lord's heart to see new people come into His kingdom, cell multiplication will be a great joy as the kingdom of God continues to grow through our cell groups.

How Many People Should be in a Cell Group?

Jesus' cell group consisted of twelve disciples. Moses encouraged small groups of ten. Ten to twelve adults in a cell seems to be an ideal number of people to serve together. New cell groups only need a few people to start. If two or three gather in His name, He is in their midst! When the group grows to twenty or more, the group can become a bit too large to be effective. The key to starting new groups is leadership. If leadership is not adequately prepared to start a new cell group, wait until leaders are properly equipped. People who are involved in cells without clear leadership often become disillusioned.

One of our cell groups a few years back had more than eighty people in it. That cell group was larger than the average church in America! But we had to wait until leadership was released for the cell group to multiply.

When a home group becomes large, another unforeseen problem may come into existence. Where do you park all the cars when you meet together as a cell at someone's home residence? Often the overflow spills onto the side of the street or road and can be a potential problem for neighbors. In this case, we suggest that cell members car pool whenever possible. Respect for the community must always be observed. Cars should never be parked where they interfere with traffic flow or neighbors' properties.

Dissolving a Cell Group

To maintain healthy cells, everyone realizes that the cell will eventually need to multiply. Even so, there have been times when a group has been together for quite some time without multiplying and finds it hard to keep an outward focus. They are satisfied with their experiences of mutual support and forget their mission to reach out beyond themselves. The closer I look at my face in the mirror each morning, the more imperfections that I see. The same principle applies to the church. If we just sit around and look at each other and forget our mission to reach the lost, we can quickly begin to dwell on the imperfections that we see in one another. This will inevitably lead us down a road of disillusionment and destruction in a cell group setting.

When a cell leader and others in the cell sense they have become spiritually stagnant, with no one desiring to multiply another cell from the parent one, they often realize they must dissolve or discontinue altogether. It is important to have the local pastor involved in the process of a cell group that dissolves. He has the grace and experience to help the cell members to quickly find their place in another cell group before the enemy can sow seeds of discouragement and confusion into their lives.

Sometimes when a cell group dissolves, it takes a period of time for believers to get involved in another cell. The local pastor may start a "transition cell group" that he leads temporarily to support God's people and help them discern their future cell group involvement.

Commissionings

Whenever someone in the home cell group is going out on a missions trip, or into a ministry, or moving to another cell or area, the entire cell should have a part in commissioning them out. This commissioning should not take place on the spur of the moment. It should be announced well in advance so that no one is taken by surprise. During the time of commissioning, have the members lay hands on the person or persons, and as many as are led by the Lord should pray. At this time, prophecy and words of wisdom and knowledge may also be given.

Commissionings are also encouraged when multiplying a new home cell group or when confirming new cell leaders or assistant leaders from within the group. Communication with the section leader and local pastor prior to this is important. If the pastor or section leader can be involved in the commissioning, it gives the Lord's people a sense of being linked to a movement of God, not just to a small group of people.

We believe that many Christians in the future will see the church as believers meeting in clusters of home cell groups in a given locality. These clusters of cell groups would network together with other congregations to affect their communities for Jesus Christ. By concentrating on relationships rather than structure, home cell groups give everyone an opportunity to be involved and people feel like they are part of a family. Like families, cell groups are not immune to problems. In the next chapter, we will take a look at some problems that may occur and give cell leaders possible solutions.

Questions to think about
from Chapter Nine

1. Contrast being "unprepared" and being "led by the Holy Spirit."

2. In what ways might a cell group meet the needs of its members?

3. How can a cell encourage members to step out in faith and practice spiritual gifts?

4. What can a cell do to minister to the children?

5. Why is it better to use the term "multiply" rather than "split" or "divide"?

CHAPTER 10

HELP!
I'M A CELL GROUP LEADER

All of us experience times of crisis. This is an opportune time for the cell group to get actively involved in the work of ministry. If you are a cell leader and someone in your cell group is going through a crisis, you should activate the members of your home cell group to serve the person as you see appropriate.

When a storm brought a huge tree crashing down on their house roof, one family at our church experienced God's love in action through their cell group. "Love started flowing our way the very next day in the form of a tub of brownies from a cell member," they reported. "Brownies don't solve a mess, but they sure lift your spirits!" Cell members came immediately to remove the tree from the roof. One evening everyone from the cell helped to repair water damage to the inside of the house. They hung a drop ceiling, painted, fixed a door, did electrical work and many other smaller jobs. This family's misfortune was turned to a blessing as cell members had the opportunity to "do it unto Jesus" as they helped bear each other's burdens.

During times of crisis or change in someone's life, it's important to respond with an attitude of love, gentleness, and compassion. A storm-torn house, change of jobs, the death of a loved one, moving, the birth of a baby, are all types of change that add extra pressures to our lives.

Remember, faith works by love. As you identify with the person's situation, God will show you how to best respond. The Lord has called us to all work together to build the body of Christ.

Practical Tips

Here are a few examples of what you can do when someone in your cell group is going through the following crisis or change:

•**Hospitalization**—provide prayer, visitation, calls to family, flowers, child care, house sitting. Contact the local pastor to let him know of the hospitalization, especially in the case of an extended or serious illness.

• **Illness**—If a person is absent from the home group meeting due to illness, the entire home cell group should be encouraged to be involved in prayer for the sick, visiting, taking meals to the family, providing transportation, sending cards and flowers.

• **Financial need**—If someone has a financial or material need, you may want to initiate a special offering to help meet the need. If it is greater than the home group can meet, the need should be discussed with your local pastor. As I mentioned before, in our church each local congregation has a "deacon's fund." This fund receives a percentage of the monies that are given to the church through the weekly tithes as well as special designated offerings. All monies that are in the deacon's fund are set apart to help those who have special financial needs, and these funds are administered through the cell group, which provides a sense of accountability.

• **Moving**—When someone moves, the home cell leader sets the standard as a servant and gives leadership to the others within the cell group who are assisting in the moving of a family or a single person from one location to another. Encourage the group to assist with packing, moving, child care and meals. It can be a great time of fellowship for your cell group! The responsibility for organizing the moving day, including helping to line up trucks, should be delegated to others within the cell group as much as is possible; however, the cell leader should take the responsibility to make sure that it happens.

• **Death in the family**—Be sensitive to the needs of the family. Pray for them and serve wherever you can. In our church, local pastors will serve with the cell leader during these times of crisis. Due to the cell leader's close relationship with the family that has experienced a death, he may receive the information before the local pastor. If this happens, cell leaders are encouraged to contact the local pastor immediately. Cell leaders are encouraged to ask the local pastor how the cell group can effectively under-gird the family during this time.

• **New baby**—Set up a schedule to provide meals for the family. Perhaps you can baby-sit some of the other children in the family during this time and set up a schedule for others within the cell to serve in this way. Again, the cell leader may find out about the new baby before the local pastor receives the information. We encourage the cell leader to be sure to contact the local pastor with this information immediately.

• **Person with a life-controlling problem**—You may want to contact your local pastor for assistance and training for a particular problem. Each of us is an able minister of the new covenant and can be used of the Lord to minister His healing; however, there are times when the Lord may want to use someone else within the body who has a special anointing in this area of healing. There also may be a special need for emotional healing or deliverance.

Delegate, Delegate, Delegate

Many cell leaders find it hard to delegate and then end up doing most of the work themselves. There are two major problems with not delegating to others. First of all, cell leaders who do not delegate sometimes get overwhelmed with their responsibilities as a home cell group leader. And secondly, if the cell leader does everything himself, the others in the cell group miss out on the blessing of serving, learning new responsibilities, and exercising their spiritual gifts.

Sometimes cell leaders tend to do things themselves because of past experiences of being turned down when they asked others to fulfill a certain responsibility. Or perhaps the person the responsibility was delegated to did his job so poorly that the cell group leader spent more time cleaning up the mess than if he would have done the whole thing himself. But if we do not give others responsibilities, how will they ever have the opportunity to learn?

Before we delegate a certain responsibility to a cell member, we need to be sure that we have trained them in this responsibility. Don't take it for granted that they know what to do. They may need coaching. For example, if you ask a cell member to care for the children, be sure that he knows what is expected of him. Otherwise you will abdicate instead of delegate. Abdication sows seeds of frustration for everyone.

Remember, delegate everything that you possibly can. Work yourself out of a job. As others increase in responsibility, you can begin to decrease and move on to the next thing the Lord has for you to do.

Dealing With Difficult Problems

Cell group leadership is not an easy responsibility, but it is rewarding. When someone in a home cell group has problems which the cell group leader feels are too intense for him to handle, we encourage him to contact his section leader or local pastor. The cell leader allows him to deal with the situation and remain available to follow through with any assistance that may be needed.

Next to prayer, the person experiencing the difficulty needs a friend. As the cell leader, take this opportunity to be a friend to the one in trouble, building a deeper relationship with that person.

Problems in the area of alcohol, drugs, physical abuse, finances, health, etc. may require a counselor who can relate to those areas specifically. Pastors and counselors who have been delivered from a particular bondage often are called to minister to others with that same problem. We have a counseling resource department at our church to resource cell group leaders and pastors with difficult situations. The section leaders or local pastors help put the cell group leader in touch with the appropriate person.

When helping someone work through a difficulty, we believe it is important to never counsel the opposite sex alone. As much as possible, men should counsel men and women counsel women. If it is necessary to counsel someone of the opposite sex, always have a third party present. This will avert temptation, the appearance of evil, or any opportunity for gossip or false accusations.

Emotional Dependency [17]

There may be times when we find that certain persons who are in the cell group are constantly draining us of our time and energy in a way that is not best for them or us. This is often called emotional dependency.

Sometimes due to the past patterns that we developed before knowing Christ, or due to our family of origin or possibly even from some wrong spiritual teaching, we develop the dysfunctional pattern of using others to meet our needs. Everyone desires to be loved and valued. Often, we overstep our boundaries when we attempt to meet those needs solely through others or when others desire the same from us.

You may find a person attracted to your cell group or to you as a leader because the basic needs of love and acceptance, security and intimacy are unmet in his life. These are legitimate needs, and while it is true that the home group can provide love, support and acceptance, it is not appropriate that the cell or cell leader become the sole source to meet these needs. The natural outgrowth of relationships developing within the cell will provide for some emotional needs but can never replace the natural family, parents, or a spouse. While the home group provides support, it is not a "support group" like Alcoholic Anonymous. We overstep our boundaries when we find ourselves wanting to provide for the security or intimacy needs of another.

Let me share an example which I believe exhibited emotional dependency. Sally started coming to one of our home groups with her two children. In the very first cell meeting, Sally began manipulating the group by sharing her needs about her truck driving husband. Apparently he was gone most of the week and left Sally to run the household. Her children were totally out of control (starved for consistent Godly discipline, you might say), and it was obvious that Sally was not looking to give anything to the group, but rather, to receive from it. In time, we discovered that she needed baby-sitters, help with her marriage, and help with their finances. She began to spend hours of time with various women in the cell usually by unannounced "drop-ins." Sally did not show a desire to come closer to Jesus or be discipled. What she did desire was to have the uncomfortable things in her life "fixed" by the caretakers and responsible ones within the cell. Sally wanted to be rescued and cared for.

The truth is that we could give and give to Sally and her family (which we initially attempted to do), but nothing or no one could fill the emotional void in her life. Recognizing this from the beginning could have spared many well-meaning people from becoming burned out.

Then what do we do with verses such as Luke 6:38, "Give and it shall be given" and Matthew 10:8, "Freely you have received, freely give . . . "? Here are some questions you can ask yourself. These same questions could be applied to help the one displaying emotionally dependent behavior.

• Am I in relation with this person or is this person in relation with me or the cell as an approval-seeker?

• Do I feel overly responsible for this person? Is it Christ-given compassion or is it guilt-filled sympathy?

• When I'm around this person do I feel as though they are looking to me to provide for their need of security and relational intimacy?

• Am I, or is this person looking to this relationship for identity?

To the woman at the well, Jesus truthfully responded, "You are right when you say you have no husband. The fact is, you have had five husbands, and the man you now have is not your husband" (John 4:17-18 NIV). Jesus did not become this woman's emotional rescuer. He let her know that He knew her life-style and situation. In verse 26, He then revealed to her, ". . . I who speak to you am he [the Messiah]."

To the man at the pool of Bethesda, an invalid for 38 years, perhaps quite dependent upon his condition and surroundings, He asked, ". . . Do you want to be made well?" (John 5:6).

Remember, we are not the savior. We do not need to meet needs or find needs in order to be important in the kingdom. We are important to Jesus before we *do* anything. The newborn baby does not meet needs; it only has needs, yet the parent loves, accepts, and approves of that child. In the same way, God loves and approves of us. Rather than forming dependent relationships with one another, we need to look to Jesus and lead others to look to Him also. [18]

Codependency

Codependency is not to be confused with emotional dependency and the terms should not be interchangeably used. Whereas emotional dependency has to do with placing any human relationship before our relationship with God (which is idolatry), codependency relates more to our need to help, fix, enable or control one with a life-controlling need.

Why is the topic of codependency and cell leadership so important? Leanne Payne in her book, *Restoring the Christian Soul Through Healing Prayer,* wrote that Christians in their zeal to serve others may actually mistake humility for idolatry by enabling sick and sinful behavior in the ones whom they are serving. [19]

Plainly and simply, cell leaders desire their cell members to be whole spiritually, physically and emotionally. When they are not whole there can be a strong tendency to become the "caretaker."

Let's define what we mean by codependency. Early on, the term codependency related to the spouse, child, or some significant person who was closely involved in the family system of one who was chemically dependent. For example: If mom is addicted to prescription drugs, it will undoubtedly affect the whole family. It will affect the finances, the marriage relationship and the relationship with the children. Mom will have good days and bad days. She may forget appointments. Mother becomes the dependent one while the remainder of the family becomes codependent.

Today, the term has evolved to mean something far beyond this definition. However, for the scope of this book, we will be dealing with the issues of "care-taking" or "over-responsibility" within the home cell group.

Cell group leaders are often confronted with people in need. Let's say that the Broad Street home cell group has been reaching out to the Johns family. Mr. Johns is an alcoholic. He spends his paycheck on alcohol and Mrs. Johns must pay all the household bills and feed her family of five on $100 per week. Consequently, she often finds herself in need of help.

Mrs. Johns shares her needs with the cell group, but has a tendency to cover-up her husband's drinking. Perhaps she even blames the problem on her husband's low-paying job. Of course the cell group wants to help. The children need food and Mrs. Johns needs to be delivered of all the financial pressure. It certainly seems right to help in whatever way necessary.

Codependency causes us to lose our objectivity and take on a warped sense of responsibility. How long can the Broad Street cell help? Perhaps to answer this question, we should ask another. How long can Mr. Johns be an alcoholic?

Mr. Johns' addiction is controlling his family. His wife wants to be rescued, helped, fixed. But, enabling this family to function normally while Mr. Johns remains addicted is very unhealthy. By *enabling*, I mean being involved in behavior that helps to relieve the pain of the consequences of addiction. Relieving pain, however, may not be helping anyone.

When cell leaders or cell members begin desiring their worth from what they do for others, they are displaying characteristics of codependency. No matter how much is done, it will never be enough. That guilt will still be there. Their attempts to please others are designed to win approval and acceptance.

How then do we help the Johns family? Perhaps we can start with the practical, immediate needs of food, finances, etc. But, finances are not the ongoing need. Mr. Johns needs Jesus and lots of healing. Until he comes to Christ, Mrs. Johns really needs to be confronted with the truth. Her covering up for Mr. Johns is codependent behavior. She needs to be honest with herself, her feelings, her children, her cell group, her husband. Denial never changes a thing.

And for cell leaders or cell members who have a tendency to enable and rescue, an identity in Christ is the answer. Such scriptures as Romans 8:1, 17, 33, 35-39; Ephesians 1:22; Colossians 3:12 and many others describe who we are in Christ.

Maintaining proper beliefs as discussed in the emotional dependency section is very important. As long as the cell helps around the Johns' house, clothes the children and pays the overdue bills, Mr. Johns can continue in his addiction and Mrs. Johns will never have to face the truth. As "Focus on the Family" founder, Dr. James Dobson appropriately says, " At times, love must be tough."

Divisiveness in the Cell Group

Paul, the apostle, gives us a strong admonition regarding those who are divisive in the church:

> *But avoid foolish disputes, genealogies, contentions, and strivings about the law; for they are unprofitable and useless. Reject a divisive man after the first and second admonition, knowing that such a person is warped and sinning, being self-condemned (Titus 3:9-11).*

A divisive spirit can do more harm in a church than anything else that I can think of. It is usually cloaked with superspiritual terminology like, "Do you really think our cell leader or our pastor is anointed by the Lord to give the type of leadership that we need?" A divisive spirit will creep into a cell group or a church like cancer. That is why Paul speaks so harshly about it.

If you are a cell group leader and someone in the group is being divisive, don't waste any time. Go to him in love and confront the situation. God hates division, and we need to hate it as much as He does. Show him what the Scriptures say about being divisive.

Some time ago, one of the men in our church began to sow seeds of discontent. He was giving his opinion about how he differed with some of the decisions that the church leadership was making. It was done in a way that was not constructive. Some of the Lord's people were confused. His actions were also causing strain on our relationship. When I realized what was happening, I faced my fears of confrontation and sat down with this brother in Christ and told him what I was seeing. He received my admonition, and today our relationship is restored.

Church Discipline

In I Corinthians 5, and Matthew 18:15-20, there are explicit instructions for dealing with serious problems in the church. People must be confronted with their sins, but always in the compassionate love of Christ. If Tom, a fellow cell member, is overcome by a sin, we should first pray for him and allow the Spirit of God to give us a heart of genuine compassion for him. According to Matthew 18, we should talk with him alone about the sin. If he does not receive us, then we should take someone with us and talk to him again. This could be someone in the home cell group, the section leader, a local pastor, or another Christian friend.

At this point, if Tom does not receive the admonition of the local church, the Scripture tells us that we should not consider him as a believer in Jesus Christ. If we get to this last step with Tom, and he does not turn from his sin, a local pastor should definitely be involved in helping to deal with the situation.

We believe this type of Scriptural church discipline is most effectively handled in the cell church setting. We are instructed in Matthew 18 and in I Corinthians 5 to take these matters to the church. The church that meets in the home provides the proper spiritual setting. In the cell group, there is a deep sense of love and compassion for Tom, because we know him.

If Tom repents, it will be a great joy for the cell group to see Tom come back into a proper relationship with the Lord. The goal of all discipline is future restoration. Restoration will only be effective if done in a spirit of gentleness. God calls Christian leaders, as servant leaders, to restore someone, not by domineering, but by sharing the truth in love.

> *"Brethren, if a man is overtaken in any trespass, you who are spiritual restore such a one in a spirit of gentleness, considering yourself lest you also be tempted" (Galatians 6:1).*

The local pastors have special grace on their lives to help cell group leaders handle church discipline situations in a Godly, compassionate way.

Vows of Confidentiality

As leaders, there have been times in the past when we have fallen into the trap of promising to not divulge information that was given to us in confidence, when in reality, it would have been much better for everyone involved to share this information with others. The Scriptures tell us in Proverbs 6:2,

> *You are snared by the words of your mouth; You are taken by the words of your mouth.*

If Bill tells us personal information and asks us to promise not to tell anyone, our response must be, "I will only do what is the most loving thing that I can do for you and for anyone else involved, and what is best for the Lord's kingdom." If Bill doesn't trust me enough to allow me to get help for him when he needs it, it is best for him not to divulge personal information. Basic confidentiality is important, but vows of confidentiality should be avoided.

Taking this approach will keep you from being ensnared by the words of your mouth. In other words, you will not be stuck with private information that you know you must share with others who could be a part of the problem or the solution but feel unable to share because of a promise of confidentiality.

Now that you've been given some advice on how to deal with potential problem areas in the cell group, I want to concentrate in the next chapter on every cell leader's commitment to Jesus Christ, to those he serves, to his church's vision, and on his commitment to flexibility so that the cell group may flow together in unity.

Questions to think about
from Chapter Ten

1. List some practical ways that cell churches can help members.

2. Why should members of a cell take turns at cell responsibilities?

3. Should a cell group respond to a difficult problem? Give examples.

4. How can you test a relationship to decide whether it is "providing support" or is a "support group"?

5. How do you handle one who gossips or rails against a leader?

6. What are the steps to restore one back into fellowship?

CHAPTER 11

A CELL LEADER'S COMMITMENT

If anyone would come after me, he must deny himself and take up his cross and follow me (Matthew 16:24 NIV). If you hold to my teaching, you are really my disciples. Then you will know the truth, and the truth will set you free (John 8:31-32 NIV). I have hidden your word in my heart that I might not sin against you (Psalm 119:11 NIV).

First and foremost, our commitment must be total surrender to Jesus Christ as Lord and Master and living a life in accordance to the Word of God. There can be no compromise. The church is built on Jesus Christ. Although relationships, believers knit together in cell groups, and all of our plans to reach the lost are important, they are secondary to our relationship with Jesus.

Commitment To The Church

Then those who gladly received his word were baptized; and that day about three thousand souls were added to them. And they continued steadfastly in the apostles' doctrine and fellowship, in the breaking of bread, and in prayers (Acts 2:41- 42).

The church is people in relationship with God and with each other, within the framework of a local expression of the body of Christ. It is not commitment to a building made of bricks and mortar. To be committed to our local body literally means we are willing to be totally sold out to Jesus and to be an active participant with other believers in a specific home cell group.

The cell leader's life is an example to other cell members how to be actively involved in the lives of people. This includes showing an interest in the people and getting together with them on occasions other than the home cell group meeting. Cell meetings are great, but real community usually happens outside the cell meetings. Any cell leader who depends only on meetings to minister and build relationships with the people the Lord has given him responsibility for is destined for failure.

People are looking for reality. Real life is not confined to meetings. It happens as we work together, play tennis together, pray together, fix the car together, bake cookies together, witness together, and eat together. The list of things we can do together is endless. This is the stuff real church is made of.

Commitment To The Vision Of The Church

Let us fix our eyes on Jesus, the author and perfecter of our faith, who for the joy set before him endured the cross, scorning its shame, and sat down at the right hand of the throne of God (Hebrews 12:2 NIV).

Jesus had a personal vision. Therefore, He endured the cross. Every business, every family, every person, every church should have a vision. Just as those who are married verbalize their commitment to their spouse by saying, "I love you," we need to verbalize our commitment to support the vision that the Lord has given to us as a local church.

We must caution, however: Exalting our church's vision above Jesus will lead to idolatry. God is the ultimate visionary, and we are created in His image. We are given the potential to dream and have visions. If we shift our primary focus from Jesus to our vision, we'll become ensnared.

Many times during the past thirteen years I have had to refocus my vision and energies to my relationship with Jesus first and then to the vision that the Lord has given to us as a church. John the apostle tells us in I John 5:21, "Little children, keep yourselves from idols." Idolatry can be so subtle that we can be ensnared by it before we know what has happened. When we begin to emphasize the vision that the Lord has given to us more than we emphasize our relationship with Jesus, we create an idol in our hearts. Ezekiel the prophet tells us, "Son of man, these men have set up their idols in their hearts, and put before them that which causes them to stumble into iniquity . . . (Ezekiel 14:3).

Even a God-inspired vision, when given preeminence above the Lord Himself, will cause us to stumble. One of the dangers of having a good cell structure, is that we can trust the structure more than the Holy Spirit. Jesus will share His glory with no other. It can be so subtle, but a good cell group vision, even though it has been birthed by the Holy Spirit, can divert us from a simple love for and devotion to Jesus. We have learned through experience that focusing on a cell group vision and structure more than focusing on Jesus produces spiritual barrenness. Only a relationship with Jesus produces life. We must stay tender before the Lord, and fellowship with Him.

It is important for the cell leader to both understand and articulate the vision of the local church and then share it with the cell group regularly. It has been said that every church must have a compelling vision (who we really are), a defined mission (what is our purpose), and a well laid out plan (how are we going to do it).

The vision and mission that the Lord has given to DOVE Christian Fellowship has been written down in the form of a vision statement, a mission statement and a plan. (See the appendix at the end of the book for our church's statements.)

Commitment To Goals

> *I press on toward the goal to win the prize for which God has called me heavenward in Christ Jesus (Philippians 3:14 NIV).*
>
> *Therefore I do not run like a man running aimlessly; I do not fight like a man beating the air (I Corinthians 9:26 NIV).*
>
> *"For I know the plans I have for you," declares the Lord, "plans to prosper you and not to harm you, plans to give you hope and a future" (Jeremiah 29:11 NIV).*

A goal is a statement of faith, a course of action. Jesus is returning to this earth. It is a goal that He has fixed. God has goals for His body and for each of us individually. We, like the apostle Paul, must run toward those goals that God has set before us.

Every cell group needs clear, attainable goals. It's also essential for each cell group leader to have clear goals. Ask the Lord what goals He wants you to set for yourself as a cell group leader. God's plan is to use each of us to set goals under the Holy Spirit's direction to change the world in which we live.

If you have a goal to pray for each member of your cell group every day, don't just say you will pray every day. Set a specific goal that is clear, measurable and attainable. For example, decide to pray one minute a day for each person and progress from there.

As you set goals as a cell group, try to involve as many persons in the cell as possible in the process. This way the whole cell group will feel a sense of responsibility for these goals to be reached. If you implement new goals and ideas too fast, the group may feel lost.

I grew up as a farm boy. During the fall of every year we dug our sweet potatoes for the winter. We placed these sweet potatoes in baskets and put them on a truck. Then came the excitement of driving the farm truck filled with sweet potatoes from the field to the house. Driving that old pick up truck was a real art. We had to round the corners very slowly or we would upset the whole load of sweet potatoes. In the same way, when we make spiritual decisions that will affect others, we need to give them enough time to know that they are a part of the decision making process so that they don't "fall off the truck." Discuss new ideas with those in your cell group before making final decisions. You are called as a team to see the kingdom of God built together.

Get away to pray, so the goals you set are not natural goals, but goals that are birthed by the Holy Spirit. Perhaps the Lord will make it clear to you that you should believe Him to see a family saved within the next two months. Or perhaps you will have as a goal to spend a certain amount of time together in prayer each week. Ask the Lord for a practical goal regarding cell group multiplication. There is an old saying, "If you fail to plan, you plan to fail!"

May I interject a word of caution concerning goals? To not reach your goal may not necessarily be failure. On the other hand, to reach your goal may not be success. Ministry to the Lord and to people must be the ultimate goal!

Commitment to Be Willing To Change

*The wind blows where it wishes, and you hear the sound
of it, but cannot tell where it comes from and where it goes.
So is everyone who is born of the Spirit (John 3:8).*

*For as many as are led by the Spirit of God, these are sons
of God (Romans 8:14).*

The only thing that is constant on this earth is the Word of
God and change. It is a bit unnerving, but true. As we truly
follow the leading of the Holy Spirit, we will continue to
change. Our cell groups will change, and each of us will continue to change as we mature in Christ. Our ways of thinking
must also change.

Years ago, during the early days of my involvement in a
para-church youth ministry, young people giving their lives
to Jesus wanted to be baptized in water as new believers. Back
then, most people seemed to be under the impression that only
the pastor or bishop of a church could perform baptisms. So
we had to look high and low to find a pastor who was willing
to baptize these new believers even though they were not yet
ready to become "members" of his congregation. We found
ourselves swimming upstream, cutting across the Christian culture of our community. It was change. Today, new believers
are baptized by "lay people" in swimming pools and bathtubs. It is accepted.

Right now, those who build according to an underground
pattern in small groups may find themselves swimming upstream. But if the Lord tarries, the church of Jesus Christ may
look so different ten years from now, we may hardly recognize
it. The Lord has called us to change!

Change is hard for most of us. But if we are going to grow
and mature, we must constantly be ready to embrace change.
For example, the change that takes place when a cell group
multiplies is not easy for the majority of us. And as leaders,
we must help others get ready for the change. It often helps
God's people when they realize that even leaders do not necessarily feel like changing, but they understand that change is
simply a part of normal church life.

We are naturally resistant to change. Human nature has
always resisted change. A case in point is the following letter
written by Martin Van Buren, then governor of New York, to

President Jackson, concerning an "evil" new business enter-
prise threatening our nation:

> January 31, 1829
> To President Jackson,
> The canal system of this country is being threatened by
> the spread of a new form of transportation known as "rail-
> roads." The federal government must preserve the canals
> for the following reasons:
> 1. If canal boats are supplanted by "railroads," serious
> unemployment will result. Captains, cooks, drivers, hos-
> tlers, repairmen and lock tenders will be left without means
> of livelihood, not to mention the numerous farmers now
> employed in growing hay for the horses.
> 2. Boat builders would suffer, and towline, whip and har-
> ness makers would be left destitute.
> 3. Canal boats are absolutely essential to defend the United
> States. In the event of the expected trouble with England,
> the Erie Canal would be the only means by which we could
> ever move the supplies so vital to waging modern war.
> As you may well know, Mr. President, "railroad" car-
> riages are pulled at the enormous speed of fifteen miles per
> hour by "engines" which, in addition to endangering life
> and limb of passengers, roar and snort their way through
> the countryside, setting fire to crops, scaring the livestock
> and frightening women and children. The Almighty cer-
> tainly never intended that people should travel at such break-
> neck speed. —Martin Van Buren, Governor of New York. [20]

Isn't that an amazing story? A future president of the
United States was extremely resistant to a change that was inevitable. Nothing would stop the change that was on the horizon. It is also inevitable that the Lord has "change" in store for
His church, and nothing will stop the change that is coming in
the future.

Building the church through cell groups requires a lot of
flexibility and change. But then, that is what life is all about.
One of my friends from YWAM told me one time, "Either we
can keep everything neat and organized, or we can continue
to allow the Lord to birth new things among us. Birthing is
messy and painful, but there is life!" I vote for life. How about
you?

As the saints minister in practical ways (laying hands on the sick, casting out demons, leading people to Christ, and serving people as the opportunities arise), we must be open to change.

Seeing others come to Jesus and helping people step by step in their Christian walk—that's real life! And it happens so effectively in the small group setting. The power of God is released as small groups learn to do the work of the kingdom and stay open to change.

Commitment Card—A Tangible Way to Show Commitment

At DOVE Christian Fellowship, each person who becomes part of a home cell group is asked to make a commitment to the others in that home cell group. This is not a commitment for a lifetime. It is a commitment for the duration of their time in their present home cell group. This is a Scripturally based commitment that a person in any local church should be able to express with conviction and confidence to the others in their local church.

A card is given to each person in the cell group listing the points of commitment to be expressed. Usually at the start of a new cell or when a new member joins, the entire cell group uses this card to profess their commitment to each other. This is not seen as a bondage but as a privilege.

The commitment card states:

> *I confess Jesus Christ as Lord. I am therefore committed to living in obedience to the Word of God and the Holy Spirit, and to being part of the church that Jesus is building throughout the world. I specifically commit myself to the body of Christ here at DOVE. I will be accountable to my brothers and sisters in the way I live my Christian life, and will support the leadership that God raises up and the vision God gives His body.*

Our commitment is to Jesus and His Word, to His body at large, and to the local expression of the body of Christ that the Lord has placed us in. Every local church has four basic characteristics.

1. Each person has a relationship with God through Jesus Christ.
2. Each person has a relationship with others in their local church.
3. There is clear leadership recognized among the people.
4. There is a common vision.

We believe that these four characteristics are a proper assessment of the local church. We are not only committed to Jesus and the church universally, but also to the leadership and the specific vision that the Lord has given to a local body. This can be expressed and lived out practically in a home cell group.

> *And we urge you, brethren, to recognize those who labor among you, and are over you in the Lord and admonish you, and to esteem them very highly in love for their work's sake. Be at peace among yourselves (1 Thessalonians 5:12-13).*
>
> *Obey those who rule over you, and be submissive, for they watch out for your souls, as those who must give account. Let them do so with joy and not with grief, for that would be unprofitable for you (Hebrews 13:17).*

Building Unity

The Scriptures place a high priority on unity.

> *How good and pleasant it is when brothers live together in unity! (Psalm 133:1 NIV).*
>
> *I appeal to you, brothers, in the name of our Lord Jesus Christ, that all of you agree with one another so that there may be no divisions among you and that you may be perfectly united in mind and thought (I Corinthians 1:10 NIV).*
>
> *... bearing with one another in love. Make every effort to keep the unity of the Spirit through the bond of peace (Ephesians 4: 2-3 NIV).*
>
> *There is one body and one Spirit—just as you were called to one hope when you were called—one Lord, one faith, one baptism; one God and Father of all, who is over all and through all and in all (Ephesians 4:4-6 NIV).*

When the people in a cell work together and flow with the Holy Spirit, there is unity and single-mindedness of purpose. As the cell leaders and other church leaders walk together in unity, the entire church is in unity together. As the leadership of one local church works in unity with the other local church leaders, the entire body of Christ in that locality experiences a bond of unity together. That is when God commands a blessing!

It has often been said that prayer and unity are the two main ingredients for revival. The cell leader will set the pace for unity and prayer in the cell group where he serves. If the cell leader is not in unity with the other leadership of the church, he should not be in cell group leadership. Remember, unity does not mean that everyone agrees on everything. I have never met two people who totally agree on everything. However, true unity means that a group of people are going in the same basic direction, are preferring one another, and are flowing with the spiritual leadership that the Lord has raised up among them.

How did God raise up spiritual leadership in the New Testament church? In the next chapter, we will take a look at two groups of leaders who oversee and serve the church—apostles and elders.

Questions to think about
from Chapter Eleven

1.   What is your local church's vision and mission?

2.   How can you help to implement this vision?

3.   Change is healthy. In what ways do you resist change?

4.   Describe the four basic characteristics of local churches.

CHAPTER 12

New Testament Church Leadership

In order for the church to be built from house to house according to an underground pattern, we need to take a fresh look at the Scriptures for a clearer understanding about church leadership. For example, since it has been so widely accepted throughout the world that the normal way to build the church is to find a pastor, a building and to start filling the pews, this philosophy has also influenced our understanding of church leadership.

Apostles and Elders

When we study the Scriptures and look closely at the New Testament, we do not see a pastor-building mentality. Instead, we see two basic groups of governmental leaders who oversee and serve the churches who meet in homes and gather together corporately at the temple, or the school of Tyrannus (Acts 19:9), or wherever else they can find to meet. Apostles and elders comprised these two groups of leaders found in Acts 15:4,

*And when they had come to Jerusalem, they were received by the church and the **apostles and the elders**; and they reported all things that God had done with them.*

Paul and Barnabas were having some problems with Jewish converts who were placing restrictions on the Gentile believers. Paul and Barnabas were convinced that these teachers from Judea were teaching a doctrine that was not according to faith, and that it would greatly hinder the work of God. So Paul and Barnabas went up to Jerusalem.

*Therefore, when Paul and Barnabas had no small dissension and dispute with them, they determined that Paul and Barnabas and certain others of them should go up to Jerusalem, to the **apostles and elders,** about this question (Acts 15:2).*

It is interesting that after they shared their testimonies with the church, they then met with the leaders of the New Testament church—the apostles and the elders:

*Now the **apostles and elders** came together to consider this matter (Acts 15:6).*

It is clear that the apostles were not necessarily the original twelve (although some of them were probably involved), but they met with the "new" apostles and the elders of the church. James appears to be the one who gave oversight to the apostles and elders in Jerusalem. He seemed to be the apostle who was responsible for the decision-making process. The next step was to send out men from their company to the church throughout the known world, exhort them, and teach them:

*And after they had become silent, James answered, saying, "Men and brethren, listen to me. . ." (Acts 15:13). Then it pleased the **apostles and elders,** with the whole church, to send chosen men of their own company to Antioch with Paul and Barnabas, namely, Judas who was also named Barsabas, and Silas, leading men among the brethren (Acts 15:22). And as they went through the cities, they delivered to them the decrees to keep, which were determined by the **apostles and elders** at Jerusalem (Acts 16:4).*

Regardless of the terminology that today's church uses for leadership, there is a need for local leaders (elders) and leaders who have a larger sphere of spiritual responsibility (apostolic overseers). Paul the apostle, wrote to Titus and exhorted him to appoint elders in every city on the island of Crete.

For this reason I left you [Titus] in Crete, that you should set in order the things that are lacking, and appoint elders in every city as I commanded you (Titus 1:5).

In order to see the church built from house to house in the nations of the world, we have come to believe that we must allow the Lord to raise up among us those with an apostolic type ministry (those who oversee larger areas) and elders who serve in every city (local area).

Apostles

According to the New Testament, apostles are "foundation layers." These apostles also seemed to be gifted to give spiritual counsel, admonition, and oversight to local leadership teams. Many of Paul's letters serve as an example of the apostolic ministry that the Lord had given to him.

> *According to the grace of God which was given to me, as a wise master builder I have laid the foundation, and another builds on it. But let each one take heed how he builds on it. For no other foundation can anyone lay than that which is laid, which is Jesus Christ (I Corinthians 3:10-11).*

Bill Scheidler, in his book *The New Testament Church and Its Ministries* gives the following insights on apostles:

> *The word "apostle" (Greek—apostolos) literally means "one who is sent forth." The word "apostle" was often used in the classical Greek world. It was used to refer to an emissary or ambassador; to a fleet of ships or an expedition sent forth with a specific objective; to the admiral who commanded the fleet or the colony which was founded by the admiral. If a fleet of ships left Rome with the purpose of establishing a new colony somewhere, all of these were called apostles— the fleet, the admiral, the new found colony.*
>
> *The particular truth that is emphasized by this usage is the relationship of those who were sent to the sender. All of these, the admiral, the fleet, and the colony that was formed, represented a true image of the one by whom they were sent. In other words, they were faithful to transmit or reflect the intentions of the sender (Hebrews 3:1). The primary attitude of a true apostle, then, must be faithfulness.* [21]

An apostle then, is one who is sent forth with authority, who faithfully represents the purposes and the intentions of the sender. There are at least 23 different apostles mentioned in the New Testament. There are also various types or classes of apostles and apostolic ministry mentioned in the Bible. For example:

1. Jesus Christ was and is the chief apostle:

> *Therefore, holy brethren, partakers of the heavenly calling, consider the Apostle and High Priest of our confession, Christ Jesus (Hebrews 3:1).*

2. The twelve apostles of the lamb:

The original twelve apostles are in a league of their own. No modern-day apostle can ever take the place of the original twelve. (Luke 6:12).

> *Now the wall of the city had twelve foundations, and on them were the names of the twelve apostles of the Lamb (Revelation 21:14).*

3. The James-type apostle:

James gave oversight to the apostles and elders in Jerusalem. He seems to have basically stayed in one location.

> *And after they had become silent, James answered, saying, "Men and brethren, listen to me" (Acts 15:13).*
> *On the following day Paul went in with us to James, and all the elders were present (Acts 21:18).*

4. The Paul-type apostle:

Paul was a traveling apostle who had been given authority and responsibility by the Lord for churches in various parts of the world.

> *Paul, an apostle of Jesus Christ by the will of God, to the saints who are in Ephesus, and faithful in Christ Jesus (Ephesians 1:1).*

It appears as if Paul was not necessarily recognized by every church as an apostle. He was, however, recognized by the churches that the Lord gave him spiritual responsibility for. He told the Corinthian Christians that his sphere of authority and responsibility included them.

> *. . . within the limits of the sphere which God appointed us—a sphere which especially includes you (II Corinthians 10:13).*

5. The Timothy-type apostle:

Timothy was sent by Paul for apostolic ministry to the Corinthian church. Although Paul was the "senior" apostle, the Corinthians also saw Timothy as having an apostolic ministry that would be used of the Lord to give them direction and guidance.

> *For this reason I have sent Timothy to you, who is my beloved and faithful son in the Lord, who will remind you of my ways in Christ, as I teach everywhere in every church (I Corinthians 4:17).*

Paul sent other men who served with him to fulfill an apostolic role in certain situations, just as he sent Timothy to Corinth. As I mentioned earlier, Paul sent Titus to Crete. Epaphras was used of the Lord to start the church in Colossae. To our knowledge, Paul never had the opportunity to go to the Colossian church personally. Nevertheless, he was still given apostolic authority from the Lord for this work. Epaphras also worked with Paul to oversee this work.

> *Epaphras, who is one of you, a bondservant of Christ, greets you, always laboring fervently for you in prayers, that you may stand perfect and complete in all the will of God (Colossians 4:12).*

6. Those involved in apostolic-type ministry:

The seventy who were sent out were involved in apostolic-type ministry. Those within a cell group who have a God-given ability to strategically plan ahead for new cells to be birthed in your city may have a "seed" of apostolic ministry developing in their lives.

I grew up with the ability to play the guitar, but it was not until I was sixteen years old that I actually started to practice and learn how to play. There are many future apostles in our midst today. They are presently being trained and groomed by the Holy Spirit to fulfill key roles in the kingdom of God in the future. An apostolic call is not something we do because we think it sounds exciting. This gift is received from the Lord and He will develop it. We believe the Lord will raise up modern day apostles to train and develop future apostles.

> Greet Andronicus and Junia, my countrymen and my fel-
> low prisoners, who are of note among the apostles, who also
> were in Christ before me (Romans 16:7).

Our current understanding is that the Lord will call many
apostolic-type overseers from the church that He is building
in this generation to serve His people. Some will serve the
church in the local area and help to oversee dozens of congregations and hundreds of cell groups. Others will go to the nations of the world to help establish and oversee new works.
Some will do both.

True apostolic overseers will have a father's heart for those
whom the Lord has placed within their sphere of spiritual responsibility. Paul told the church of the Thessalonians:

> For neither at any time did we use flattering words, as
> you know, nor a cloak for covetousness—God is witness.
> Nor did we seek glory from men, either from you or from
> others, when we might have made demands as apostles of
> Christ. But we were gentle among you, just as a nursing
> mother cherishes her own children. So, affectionately long-
> ing for you, we were well pleased to impart to you not only
> the gospel of God, but also our own lives, because you had
> become dear to us (I Thessalonians 2:5-8).

The person with a true apostolic ministry will respond to
those within his care in the same way that a father will respond to his married children. He has authority because he is
a spiritual father, however, he is careful to use that authority
in a way that will under-gird the local elders and the local
church.

DOVE Christian Fellowship International is presently encouraging the development of three spheres of leadership: cell
leaders, local church elders and apostolic leaders. The overseers of DOVE Christian Fellowship International consist of a
group of leaders who have an apostolic-type role. Every local
congregation either has a local leadership team (local elders)
or is in the process of developing it. Some persons may be involved in more than one role at the same time. James and Peter seemed to be both apostles and elders (I Peter 5:1).

Elders

When believers are sick, they are instructed by the Scriptures to call for the elders of the church. James seems to be referring to the local elders.

> *Is anyone among you sick? Let him call for the elders of the church, and let them pray over him, anointing him with oil in the name of the Lord (James 5:14).*

Paul gives clear qualifications for the appointment of elders in I Timothy 3:1-7 and Titus 1:5-9:

> *For this reason I left you in Crete, that you should set in order the things that are lacking, and appoint elders in every city as I commanded you—if a man is blameless, the husband of one wife, having faithful children not accused of dissipation or insubordination. For a bishop must be blameless, as a steward of God, not self-willed, not quick-tempered, not given to wine, not violent, not greedy for money, but hospitable, a lover of what is good, sober-minded, just, holy, self-controlled, holding fast the faithful word as he has been taught, that he may be able, by sound doctrine, both to exhort and convict those who contradict (Titus 1:5-9).*

In the New Testament, we see elders being appointed by those who give them apostolic oversight. Paul instructed Titus to appoint elders in Crete. We are told in the book of Acts that Paul and Barnabas ordained elders in every church. The qualifications for elders are mostly character qualifications, not abilities. The only ability that is mentioned in the two lists mentioned in Scripture is the ability to teach.

> *So when they had appointed elders in every church, and prayed with fasting, they commended them to the Lord in whom they had believed (Acts 14:23).*

Serving as an elder in the local church is both a privilege as well as a serious responsibility. Kevin Conner, in his book, *The Church In The New Testament* says:

> *If any man desire, "reach out after, long for, to covet, to stretch oneself" the office of a bishop, he should seek to qualify. It speaks of a deep inward drive or impulse to equip*

> *oneself for the ministry of an elder. It is a "good work" (I*
> *Timothy 3:1). An excellent task. It is not a desire for a title*
> *or office position, but work! Matthew 23:1-12; Job 32:21-*
> *22. Not flattering titles. The office is work! As long as one*
> *is functioning in the office and working he is such. It is not*
> *holding titular power, or power of a title.* [22]

It is our present understanding that local elders serve and oversee God's people meeting from house to house in a given area. A primary responsibility is to serve and equip the cell group leaders. They are also responsible before the Lord for the equipping and encouraging of the saints locally. The five-fold ministry (apostles, prophets, evangelists, pastors and teachers) are released by the elders to equip and encourage the saints within the congregations where they serve. Many of the elders may be functioning in the fivefold ministry. We'll be talking more about this in the next chapter.

God-Appointed Leadership

We see in the Scriptures that God appoints leadership over various spheres in His kingdom. God uses these leaders to make decisions that affect those whom they serve. These leaders are called by the Lord to lead through servanthood. For example, husbands and wives are appointed by the Lord to give leadership to their families. God speaks to the family through the father and mother who serve in leadership in the home. The husband is appointed by God as the head of his household, yet he leads as a team with his wife. He is called to lay down his life for his wife and children. A wise father and mother will listen to their children before making decisions that will affect them.

In the church, God is raising up teams of elders and teams of apostolic leaders who will pray and work together. As these teams walk together in unity and listen to the wisdom of God that comes from those whom they serve, there should be clear headship among each team. There is headship in every realm and sphere of God's kingdom. This person serves as the "primary vision carrier" for the group he is leading.

Both the Old and New Testament give numerous examples of this leadership principle. The Scriptures tell us in Numbers

27:16, "Let the Lord . . . set a man over the congregation." Although Moses worked closely with a leadership team (Aaron and Miriam), he was clearly anointed by God to lead the children of Israel. In the New Testament in Acts 13:13, we read about Paul and his party who were involved in establishing churches. In Acts 15:13-22, when the apostles and elders gathered together to make a doctrinal decision in the early church, after a time of discussion, James made the judgement as to what the decision should be. The other apostles and elders and the church confirmed the decision. Leadership in both the Old and New Testament did not work alone, but with a team of leaders who served with them. Paul and Barnabas appointed elders in every church (Acts 14:23).

It is amazing what the Lord will do when a team of people are willing to pray together and work as a team in complete unity and yet recognize Godly appointed leadership among them. We use the analogy of a head and shoulders regarding church leadership. Psalms 133 gives a clear understanding of how head and shoulders leadership and decision-making works.

> *Behold, how good and how pleasant it is for brethren to dwell together in unity! It is like the precious oil upon the head, running down on the beard, the beard of Aaron, running down on the edge of his garments. It is like the dew of Hermon, descending upon the mountains of Zion; for there the Lord commanded the blessing—life forevermore (Psalms 133:1-3).*

The head of every team needs to be properly attached to the shoulders (the others on the team) through a God-ordained relationship of trust and affirmation. If the head moves too far from the shoulders (by not honoring the team) or if the head is forced down (by the team not honoring the head), the body experiences a pain in the neck. If the head is appropriately attached to the shoulders (through relationship, trust, servanthood, prayer and proper communication), and the shoulders support and affirm the head, the oil of the Holy Spirit will run down from the head to the shoulders to the body. As these servant leaders dwell together in the unity of Christ, God will command a blessing as indicated in Psalm 133.

Decision-making

We believe that leadership teams should strive to get the mind of the Lord together through prayer and consensus whenever possible. However, there may be times when a consensus cannot be reached.

For example, Icthus Fellowship in London, England, is a church made up of 27 congregations. They have a leadership team of eight who oversee the whole church. This team sets broad policy, appoints the congregational leaders and lets them get on with leading the local congregations within the policies agreed upon by the leadership team. Although they try to reach complete agreement on every decision, they are not bound by the need for unanimity. They call this "avoiding the rule of the negative." That is, if seven agree and one disagrees, under unanimity, the negative would carry the decision. The entire team clearly recognizes Roger Forster as the apostolic leader, and after prayer and discussion if the team cannot come to complete agreement, Roger makes the decision. James the apostle seems to have had the same role in Acts 15.

These leadership principles apply to any sphere of church leadership—the corporate church, the local congregation, or the cell group. A wise leader of a congregation will always desire to involve his whole leadership team in decision-making. As the senior elder, he is responsible to discern what the Lord is saying through the team serving with him. The senior leader will assume his God-given leadership role and discern whether or not a consensus has been reached. If a decision *must* be made and there is not a complete consensus, the senior leader, after considering the input from each team member, needs to make the decision. However, the senior elder has final authority, not absolute authority. If there is conflict or an impasse in decision-making, apostolic overseers of the corporate church should provide an outside court of appeal for the senior elder and his team.

Although the final decisions affecting the local church are usually made by the eldership team, we should not forget that the wisdom of God is often manifest in God's people in the church. Church leaders are encouraged to draw from this wisdom before making decisions.

Experience God's Blessing

We have come to believe that regardless of the terminology the church at large uses today for leadership, there are local leaders (elders) and leaders who have a larger sphere of spiritual responsibility (apostolic-type overseers). We are fully persuaded at this time that both are needed in order to effectively reach an entire area for Christ. We further believe when a new cell church begins, it is necessary to allow time for growth before these two levels of leadership are established. It is spiritually healthy, though, for the leaders of the new cell church to be receiving input and counsel from a person or persons who have an apostolic call on their lives.

In the next chapter, we will discuss the role of the deacon and the fivefold ministry. Although there are many kinds of deacons, our current understanding is that the closest Scriptural example that we have of a deacon is a cell group leader. When apostolic-type overseers, elders, fivefold ministry gifts, and deacons each learn how to understand their own spheres of authority and responsibility, they can work together under the leadership of the Holy Spirit to reach the world from house to house, city to city, and nation to nation.

Questions to think about
from Chapter Twelve

1. What are the Scriptural responsibilities of apostolic overseers and elders?

2. Give a few examples from the Bible of the different types of apostolic ministry.

3. Where in the Bible are the qualifications for an elder?

CHAPTER 13

TWO MYTHS—HOLY MEN AND HOLY BUILDINGS

These were more fair-minded than those in Thessalonica,
in that they received the word with all readiness, and
searched the Scriptures daily to find out whether these things
were so (Acts 17:11).

Although it may often be hard to admit, many times we
base our theology more on our preconceived ideas and our
past experiences than we think. Many Baptists grow up with a
Baptist understanding of the Scriptures, and they are convinced
that "their" brand of theology is correct. This also applies to
the Methodists, the Lutherans, the Charismatics . . . including
you and me! So then, we need to be sure that what we believe
about the church is based on the Scriptures, and not on our
own traditional understanding of the way things have been
done in the past.

The Berean Christians refused to take everything that Paul
preached at face value. They went home and studied the Scriptures to be sure that the things that Paul was saying were really true. Is it possible that certain traditions that we consider
to be completely Scriptural, in reality, are not based on the Bible
at all? Could it be that the real reason we do these things is
because our spiritual parents and grandparents did them? We
are creatures of habit who tend to gravitate toward our own
traditions.

Did you ever hear of the young mother who always cut
the ends off of the ham before baking it in the oven? When she
was asked why she always followed this procedure she said,
"Because Grandma did it that way." Little did she know that
Grandma's roast pan was too small for the entire ham; that

was the only motivation Grandma had to cut off the ends! We need to know why we do what we do!

In the church, we constantly find ourselves following certain traditions. Some traditions are good; however, we need to be sure that our ways of thinking about the church are the same as our God's. If they are not in accordance with the thoughts of God, we are probably following dead traditions. These traditions, then, are nothing more than myths. They must be replaced by the Word of God. Otherwise, the church will never be built from house to house, city to city, and nation to nation.

We feel the following are myths that many Christians believe today which hinder the work of the Lord in this generation. We have come to believe that these myths must be replaced by the truth of God's Word.

The Holy Man Myth

Many Christians today have set up the pastor of the local church as the holy man. They have elevated the pastors and the priests as holy men who stand between them and the Lord. The Scriptures tell us that we are all kings and priests (Revelation 1:6). We all have direct access to the Lord through the shed blood of Jesus Christ.

A pastor is literally a "shepherd." He cares for the "sheep." And his caring for the sheep has nothing to do with his position, but with the gifting and calling that the Lord has placed on his life. He just loves people!

The tradition that has been established across the world today is that the leader of the local church is called "the pastor." The pastoral title has been elevated above the other ministry gifts that we find in the fourth chapter of Ephesians. This can be detrimental to the growth of God's kingdom. Here's why. The pastor becomes the "holy man," and he performs his services in a "holy building." Instead of each believer realizing that he is a vital part of the Lord's spiritual army, the believers begin to look to this "holy man" rather than the Lord. And then we give him a title—Pastor Bob or Pastor Jack.

The primary leader of the local church must be called by the Lord and anointed for leadership. He must have a shepherd's heart for God's people, even though the ministry gift in operation in his life may not be that of a pastor. If he is not a pastor himself, it's important that he has a pastor serving with him to look after the needs of the people.

Perhaps the leader of the local church is an administrator, or an evangelist, or an apostle. The real question is this: Does this person have a leadership gift and a calling from the Lord to be the primary leader of this work?

Imagine a band playing. Is the lead singer always the leader of the band? Or is the drummer the leader? Perhaps the guitarist leads. No! The leader is that person who has the ability and the "call" to lead, regardless of his ability to play a certain instrument. It is not wrong for the primary leader of the church to be called the pastor if he really is. However, if he is not a pastor, and he uses the terminology "pastor," God's people may get a wrong perception of what his true calling is. This leads to disappointment for the sheep when he is not functioning according to his title. Again, we are not saying that it is wrong to call the senior leader of a local congregation or a local church the "pastor." We just believe that it may not always be the best terminology to use. The term elder(s) may be a more Scriptural term to use.

> *For this reason I left you in Crete, that you should set in order the things that are lacking, and appoint elders in every city as I commanded you (Titus 1:5).*
>
> *So when they had appointed elders in every church, and prayed with fasting, they commended them to the Lord in whom they had believed (Acts 14:23).*
>
> *The elders who are among you I exhort, I who am a fellow elder and a witness of the sufferings of Christ, and also a partaker of the glory that will be revealed: Shepherd the flock of God which is among you, serving as overseers, not by compulsion but willingly, not for dishonest gain but eagerly; nor as being lords over those entrusted to you, but being examples to the flock (I Peter 5:1-3).*

Saints Called to do the Work of Ministry

The holy man myth tells us that the pastor is responsible for all of the ministry in the church. The truth is that the saints are called to be equipped for the work of ministry.

> *And He Himself gave some to be apostles, some prophets, some evangelists, and some pastors and teachers, for the equipping of the saints for the work of ministry, for the edifying of the body of Christ (Ephesians 4:11-12).*

Our view at present is that this myth *must* be replaced by the Word of God in order for the church to be effective today. The pastor's responsibility must be to equip the saints to minister! Thousands of pastors are burning out today due to missing this truth. They are spending the bulk of their time ministering instead of training the believers to minister. And without building on an underground pattern, it is almost impossible not to burn out! Remember, Jesus said that His yoke is easy and His burden is light. But it must be *His* burden!

For example, if there is a need for counseling, rather than automatically expecting the pastor to have all the answers, believers should allow the pastor or another qualified individual to train them. The next time they can be the ones the Lord uses to see others set free.

Another way this myth surfaces is that the "pastor" is expected to preach every Sunday. We believe the Lord's best is for the church to be built as apostles, prophets, evangelists, pastors, and teachers encourage and equip the saints from house to house and from congregation to congregation. If any of these gifts are not yet developed in your local church, bring in the ministry gifts that are needed from other parts of the body of Christ. These proven ministries will help to identify and cultivate these gifts from within your local church.

What About The Fivefold Ministry?

Our current understanding is that the fivefold ministry gifts are anointed equipping gifts given to us by Jesus Himself to train and encourage the body of Christ. They are not necessarily synonymous with governmental leadership positions, like elders. Many times these fivefold ministry gifts will serve in areas of church government; however, it is not primarily because of the ministry gift that they have, but because the Lord has called them to this area of governmental leadership.

Our view is that many of these "fivefold" ministry gifts are for trans-local ministry, not to be used solely in one cell or congregation as seen in Acts 15:22, 30-32, 35. We have come to believe that these gifts should be used from cell to cell (house to house) and from congregation to congregation as much as possible. We also acknowledge that the pastor, who has a shepherd's heart for the people in a given area may not travel as much as the other fivefold ministry gifts. Some pastors might also be pastors to pastors and then be involved in traveling ministry.

We have also discovered that most fivefold ministry gifts have a "gift mix." For example, someone may be a prophetic teacher, or a teaching evangelist. It seems to us that the apostle, prophet, evangelist, pastor and teacher must learn how to function together in order for the church of Jesus Christ to come to a place of maturity. Is it possible that much of what we have seen regarding the five gifts working together has been manufactured in the minds of man more than it has been the plan of God? We have been involved in various teams and have made sincere attempts to somehow cause these gifts to work together. We have simply not seen the fivefold ministry work properly yet. But we believe it is the will of God for the fivefold ministry to function together properly and to equip and encourage the church as the body of Christ matures in the days ahead. We await with great expectation what the Lord will reveal to us in the future.

From our limited understanding, here is one reason that we believe it hasn't worked yet. The gifts of apostle, prophet, evangelist, pastor and teacher are anointed leadership gifts for the purpose of equipping and encouraging and training the church, rather than governmental leadership positions in the body of Christ. We may have a tendency to confuse these two types of leadership in the church— anointed equipping leadership and anointed governmental leadership.

Apostles are given to the church to help us receive a vision from the Lord to reach the world. Prophets are given to train us to listen to the voice of God. Evangelists are called of

God to stir us and train us to reach the lost. Pastors are commissioned by the Lord to encourage us and show us how to make disciples! And teachers have a divine anointing to assist us in understanding the Word of God. These ministry gifts should be ministering to every level of the church: to individuals, families, cell groups, congregations, movements, and the church at large.

Will some of these fivefold ministry gifts be involved in leadership as an overseer or an elder? Of course they will. We just cannot try to program it! We are of the persuasion that the church which is going to grow is the church that makes sure they are receiving a regular impartation from each of these ministry gifts while realizing that only Jesus has all of the gifts.

This is the reason it is important for people with the various gifts to minister the Word at the cell group, the congregational gatherings, and to large corporate meetings. We need to hear from each of the five ministry gifts. If your cell group is lacking a zeal for evangelism, ask an evangelist to come to your meetings and minister to you for a few weeks. Then see if any of the believers in your cell are willing to go with him to share his faith with an unsaved person. You will be amazed at the results!

Again, preaching and teaching is not the only way we can receive an impartation from these gifts. For example, the best way to receive an impartation from a pastor may be to join him while he imparts the truth of the Word of God to someone who is in a crisis. We are confirming the need to sit under the public preaching of the Word. However, we feel that the church may have been too narrow-minded about the way we can be equipped by the fivefold ministry.

What About Deacons?

Some believers teach that deacons are no longer needed in today's church. In other Christian circles, people believe that deacons function as the leadership board of the local church. We are fully convinced at this time that literally thousands of deacons need to be released to prepare for the coming revival. These deacons are not a church governmental board, but instead, a group of servants who are released to obey the living God. A deacon is literally "a servant or a minister."

Now in those days, when the number of the disciples was multiplying, there arose a complaint against the Hebrews by the Hellenists, because their widows were neglected in the daily distribution. Then the twelve summoned the multitude of the disciples and said, "It is not desirable that we should leave the word of God and serve tables. Therefore, brethren, seek out from among you seven men of good reputation, full of the Holy Spirit and wisdom, whom we may appoint over this business; but we will give ourselves continually to prayer and to the ministry of the word." And the saying pleased the whole multitude. And they chose Stephen, a man full of faith and the Holy Spirit, and Philip, Prochorus, Nicanor, Timon, Parmenas, and Nicolas, a proselyte from Antioch, whom they set before the apostles; and when they had prayed, they laid hands on them. Then the word of God spread, and the number of the disciples multiplied greatly in Jerusalem, and a great many of the priests were obedient to the faith (Acts 6:1-7).

Likewise deacons must be reverent, not double-tongued, not given to much wine, not greedy for money . . . (I Timothy 3:8).

Deacons serve in hands-on ministry in the church. Again, we have presently come to believe that the closest Scriptural example that we have of a cell group leader is the ministry of the deacon. We are not saying that cell group leaders should be called deacons; however, we do believe there is a resemblance between New Testament deacons and cell group leaders. Although there may be many types of deacons, the cell leader seems to function in many ways as a New Testament deacon, in that he is called to practical spiritual service.

The Holy Building Myth

The church is people, or literally, "called-out ones." The buildings and meetings that are used must serve the people and the purposes of God. The people cannot be serving the building or the meeting.

We sometimes call this the "Holy Building" myth. Somehow the church today has been led to believe that the church building is a holy place. Nearly everything spiritual is supposed to center around the holy building. In reality, it is we who are believers in Jesus Christ who are holy, not a church building.

I was talking to a pastor on the staff of a large mega-church one day, and he told me that there were so many meetings and programs in the church building that the people did not have time to really minister in the cell groups that were being established from house to house. I asked this pastor, "Why don't you close down some of your midweek meetings in your building to give God's people more time to develop relationships and practical outreach in the cell groups?"

I will never forget his response. "If we stop having some of our public meetings, our offerings will go down. And if our offerings go down, the large building that we are meeting in will be used as an airplane hanger instead of a church facility." The mortgage on the building had to be paid. They were a slave to their building!

What is the first thing that you think of when someone uses the word "church"? Most of us think of a building that has been dedicated to the Lord for His people to meet in. But that is not a church! The church is people!

During one of my first trips to Scotland, I was introduced to a new term, "haggis." When I inquired about this new word, my Scottish friends decided to play a trick on me. They told me that a haggis was an animal that lived on the hills. Due to the hills being so steep, they felt that it was important for me to know that the haggis' legs were longer on one side than on the other so that they could walk on the side of mountains without falling over. Ridiculous! And yet, when I thought of the word haggis, I would visualize this animal roaming on the hills of Scotland. Later I was told the truth. Haggis was actually a food to eat, not a rare, lopsided Scottish animal!

Until we begin to visualize the church as she really is, a group of people bought by the blood of Jesus Christ, who are in a relationship with Him and with one another with a vision to reach the world, we will continue to think in terms of buildings instead of people. It is like an army thinking that the real army is the barracks instead of the soldiers!

*And I also say to you that you are Peter, and on this rock
I will build My church, and the gates of Hades shall not
prevail against it (Matthew 16:18).*

Jesus was not thinking about bricks and mortar when He
said that He would build His church. He was thinking about
His people whom He would empower with the Holy Spirit
and send from house to house into every strata of society for
the furtherance of His kingdom. Let's make a decision today
to change our way of thinking. Instead of emphasizing "going
to church," let's be the church!

Let's dream together in the next chapter about the church
truly being the church that Jesus Christ intends to come back
for!

Questions to think about
from Chapter Thirteen

1. How can we "honor" our leaders without making them into "holy men"?

2. What is the responsibility of every believer?

3. What effect do the fivefold ministry gifts have on the church?

4. How can these ministry gifts help a cell group? Congregation?

5. How is a cell leader similar to a deacon?

CHAPTER 14

LET'S DREAM TOGETHER

ev. Martin Luther King, Jr., slain civil rights leader in America, had a dream to see racial equality become a reality. I too, have a dream. I have a dream ... to see the church really be the church! I dream that the church will be the grass roots movement we have been called to be, as we serve the Lord from house to house, city to city, and nation to nation.

It Happened in a Home

I love to read the book of Acts. It seems like everywhere the apostles went, there was either a revival or a riot. Paul and Silas went to Philippi and cast a demon out of a fortune teller. Her masters were irate and threw Paul and Silas into prison. So they started singing hymns and the Lord sent an earthquake. The jailer was so shook up he was going to take his life, but Paul quickly assured him that the prisoners were all still there in the prison. Let's pick up on the story.

> *And he brought them out and said, "Sirs, what must I do to be saved?" So they said, "Believe on the Lord Jesus Christ, and you will be saved, you and your **household**." Then they spoke the word of the Lord to him and to all who were in his **house**. And he took them the same hour of the night and washed their stripes. And immediately he and all his family were baptized. Now when he had brought them into his **house**, he set food before them; and he rejoiced, having believed in God with all his **household** (Acts 16:30-34).*

These guys were amazing! Paul and Silas had just experienced imprisonment, a beating, and an earthquake. Yet they were prepared to experience a move of God, in the home of the jailer. It all happened "underground," in a home.

Rick Joyner, in his book *The Harvest*, states,

> *One of the greatest tools that the Lord will use for equipping His people will be home groups. Literally hundreds of thousands of couples will begin to open their homes to small groups. These couples will be equipped to lead the lost to Christ, cast out demons, heal the sick and lay a strong biblical foundation in the lives of new believers. These will not become isolated home churches but will be used to incorporate multitudes of new believers into larger congregations. After they have brought a group of new believers to a place of stability and function in the church they will begin with another group of new believers.*
>
> *Ultimately, home groups will become the foundation upon which the entire church is being built. Home group ministry teams will actually provide the bulk of the work in equipping the saints, including teaching and pastoring. Without these small ministry teams church leaders would be quickly overwhelmed by the massive task of the harvest.* [23]

The next revival will happen from house to house. Have you experienced a spiritual prison or a spiritual earthquake in your life during the recent past? Expect a move of God in your home and in the homes of your "oikos" during these next crucial days.

Three Kinds of Churches

Let's take a look at three types of churches that grow. First there are the mega-churches. They usually use one building that becomes the center for "ministry." In a mega-church you will usually find a clear vision and a real sense of unity as the Lord's people work together with a common purpose. Often a gifted charismatic leader is found at the helm of this type of church. The Lord has used mega-churches during the past decade in a marvelous way; however, some mega-churches may have some deficiencies.

Karen Hurston, who has spent more than ten years of her life studying churches, told me once that many mega-churches are more like teaching centers. This is a bold analysis, but in some cases she may be right. One of the difficulties that many mega-churches often have is that many believers are bench warmers and never use the many gifts that the Lord has given to them.

A second type of church that is growing is an established denominational church. One church outgrows its building, and a group is sent out to start another congregation. Praise God for many, many wonderful denominational churches today. There are also many new churches which are linked together by an "apostolic fellowship" that may be seen as a type of a denomination. The positive trait that you can find in many denominations is the freedom for each new congregation to use the gifts that it has. Many people get involved in the work of the kingdom. Some denominations have a focus on their central denominational headquarters; however, others continue to grow with little "control from the top."

One of the difficulties that some denominations have is a constant struggle between the vision of "central headquarters" and the vision of many of the local churches. When a lack of unity comes into a denominational structure, they usually lose their spiritual momentum and fervency for prayer. Believers are no longer focused on Jesus and the harvest, because they are too focused on each other. The result is spiritual barrenness.

This brings us to a third type of church that is growing—a grass roots movement. This type of church is being modeled for us in various parts of the world today. I mentioned the church in Ethiopia which is modeling this type of church. The church in China is also an example. The church in the book of Acts was a grass roots movement of the Holy Spirit as was the Methodist revival of the 1970s.

A Grass Roots Movement

All grass roots movements seem to have some common denominators. First of all, they usually meet in small groups in homes for mutual accountability and discipleship. Secondly, nearly every saint is involved in the work of ministry. Thirdly, those in leadership are often average, common people who know that they have a big God living inside of them.

> *Now when they saw the boldness of Peter and John, and perceived that they were uneducated and untrained men, they marveled. And they realized that they had been with Jesus (Acts 4:13).*

A fourth common denominator in grass roots movements seems to be an emphasis on prayer. The Moravians prayed in agreement around the clock for 100 years!

And a fifth common denominator appears to be the use of roving preachers/teachers who went from town to town and from house to house. These "circuit riders" kept the revival fire alive.

We need to look around us today. There are movements of the Holy Spirit right under our noses. YWAM and Campus Crusade for Christ are grass roots movements. They emphasize having a common vision and exhort their constituency to maintain a close relationship with Jesus and have a vision to reach the world. Is it possible that many of us in the church have been so caught up in church programs and committees that we have basically missed it? It is not too late! We believe that one of the reasons the Lord has raised up para-church ministries in these last days is to be examples of grass roots movements in this generation to show the church how it can be done. The time has come for the church of Jesus Christ to catch on to what the Lord is doing today.

Part of the secret to grass roots movements is that clusters of believers work together with a common purpose. Yet there is a tremendous amount of flexibility for each group of believers to continue to expand and work together with other groups to build the kingdom of God. Some church growth consultants today call this type of church a meta-church. Carl George, in his book, *Prepare Your Church for the Future*, says,

> *The prefix meta- means "change," as in* metabolism, meta*morphosis,* meta*physical, and the Greek word* metanoia *("to change one's mind" or "repent").* [24]

We have come to believe that a meta-church then is a grass roots movement that is constantly willing to change the structure in order to obey the Holy Spirit's direction to prepare laborers for the coming harvest.

Again, the book of Acts is an excellent example of a grass roots (or ground swell) movement as the Holy Spirit moved from house to house, city to city, and nation to nation. When the apostles and elders met in Jerusalem to make decisions on certain issues that were affecting the church, the church leaders sent the prophets and teachers back to the churches to give their verdict, teaching the Word of God and encouraging the believers (Acts 15 and 16) with the result that the church continued to grow! Some of the dangers that face grass roots movements are exclusiveness, heresy, and pride. These dangers can be eliminated if the spiritual leaders are accountable and open with leaders in other parts of the body of Christ. We need each other.

Preparing for the Future

I don't know what is in store for the future of our nation. Unless there is a genuine revival, our nation is in big trouble. What if the government closed down every church building overnight? Would the Christians that you know be able to survive without their weekly church programs?

Now is the time to prepare for the future. The church must be built from house to house! Let's put our tithe money into supporting apostles, prophets, evangelists, pastors and teachers and freeing them up to pray, study the Word, and equip the saints from house to house, city to city, and nation to nation.

I dream about the church of Jesus Christ experiencing a new flexibility in the coming days. New churches will be birthed by the Holy Spirit to provide new wineskins for the coming harvest. They will network with the church that Jesus is building throughout the world. In some cases, large homes could be used for these churches to meet in and the money that is saved on building rental and maintenance can be given to missions and to the support of the five ministry gifts that the Lord has given to equip the body of Christ. Cells could meet in smaller homes, and larger homes could be used for these celebration meetings. Every few months a large auditorium or amphitheater could be rented for a massive celebration of believers involved in cell groups throughout the area. All of the churches in a given area could begin to share their

resources and support various gifts of administrations, counseling and apostolic ministry for sending missionaries, etc.

A team of apostolic overseers would give oversight to the
church in a given area; however, they would not be involved
in the majority of the decision-making. They would only concern themselves with the basic values and guiding principles
of the Christian revival movement. Local elders would handle
the majority of the decision-making at the local level. People
would be added to the church daily as they are being saved!
And everyone would be involved in making disciples. As
someone said recently, "When revival hits, everyone will need
to be a cell leader."

As we look to the future, we can expect the Lord to teach
all of us to be flexible as we receive direction from Him. New
types of cells and congregations will spring up to take care of
the harvest. Recently, I was speaking at a seminar and met a
woman who told me she leads a cell group meeting at 12:00
midnight. She ministers to people who work the second shift!
That's flexibility!

As I said before, some congregations may meet in homes,
releasing more money for missions rather than putting it into
rent, mortgages, or maintenance. Other congregations may be
led of the Lord to purchase, rent, or build facilities for teaching
and training and to provide a place for outreach to the lost in
their communities.

We pursued the possibility of constructing a building three
or four times during the past twelve years, but the Lord closed
the door each time. However, that doesn't mean not owning a
building is more spiritual. The issue is building a structure
that accommodates the persons it is serving while maintaining a high standard of stewardship of the Lord's resources. We
need to constantly reevaluate. There may be times that too
much of the Lord's money is being spent on renting properties, when purchasing or building a facility is a better use of
the Lord's money.

Apostles, prophets, evangelists, pastors and teachers will
go from house to house and from congregation to congregation to train and encourage the saints to minister in the love
and power of our Lord Jesus Christ. Pastors will also equip
the saints to make disciples in each local area.

Local elders will serve God's people in their local congregations. Apostolic overseers would be free to spend time in prayer, in ministering the Word and continuing to give clear direction for the whole church under the anointing of the Holy Spirit. These apostolic-type overseers would lead more by influence than by hands-on management. They would be more concerned about undergirding the saints through prayer and encouragement rather than in "leading from the top."

Teams of prophets should relate to the apostolic overseers on a regular basis as they receive messages from the Lord. The apostolic giftings need the prophetic giftings to stay on track. Dick Iverson from Portland, Oregon points out that "the apostle is objective in nature, while the prophet is subjective in nature." And Kevin Conner from Melbourne, Australia confirms this by adding, "apostles and prophets are especially called to work together, each balancing the other." [25]

Small group leaders will serve in a deacon-type role, serving the people of God, and making disciples from house to house. They model New Testament hospitality. The home will be the main center for ministry.

We can expect to experience real joy as we work together as the church in each community. At certain times, hundreds of churches in a given area will close down their Sunday morning services and meet together as a sign to the world that the body of Christ is one as the Father and the Son are one. In some parts of the country, sports stadiums could be utilized for these massive celebration meetings.

As we meet weekly in local congregations and cell groups from house to house, our communities will be reached for Christ. Apostles and missionaries would continue to be sent out to the nations as churches are planted throughout the world. We will walk in the fear of the Lord and in the comfort of the Holy Spirit. The young and the old will labor together, as the Lord turns the hearts of the fathers to the children, and the hearts of the children to their fathers (Malachi 4:6).

The church will work together internationally as the Lord sovereignly ordains international networks of apostolic-type leaders. These leaders will submit to one another and build the church on the continents of the world. Modern day prophets will be assisting them in this work. There is no competition in the kingdom of God, and the church will experience a laboring together that will make the world systems around us sit up and take notice. There are various anointings and spiritual insights that believers from different nations and continents have that we all need. There is no group of believers in any one city, nation, or continent that has it all. The Lord has made His body in a way that we all need to be dependent upon one another during these last days.

This is the kind of church that I dream about and expect to experience in the coming days. It is a true "underground" church that is not dependent upon the church structures as we know them, but is a living organism that radically revolutionizes every strata of society as believers meet together from house to house with a vision burning in their hearts for the cities and the nations of this world.

Questions to think about
from Chapter Fourteen

1. Do you believe the "house to house" concept is one of the Lord's strategies to evangelize the whole world? Explain.

2. Give five common characteristics of grass-root movement church groups.

3. What is a "meta-church"?

4. What would you do if all the church buildings were closed down by the government?

5. Who should be making disciples?

CHAPTER 15

CROSSING THE
RIVER

During the spring of 1992, I was ready to quit. I felt misunderstood, and I wasn't sure if it was worth all the hassle. I told my wife LaVerne one day, "If I get kicked in the head one more time (figuratively speaking), I don't know if I can get up again."

As the senior leader of our church, I was frustrated, exhausted and overworked. God had given me a vision to be involved in building the underground church, but in the last few years we had strayed from that original vision. My immaturity as a leader, lack of training and my own inability to communicate clearly the things that God was showing me led to frustration. In a misguided attempt to please everyone, I was listening to dozens of voices who seemed to be giving conflicting advice and direction. I felt unable to get back on track. I was tired and was encouraged to take a sabbatical.

So, I took the summer off to unwind, spend time with my family, and just enjoy life. After about five weeks I really began to enjoy myself. I even got into painting and wallpapering our house. Amazing! God is still in the miracle business!

During the last few weeks of the sabbatical, I spent some extended time at a cabin in the mountains. One morning I went out for a jog, and in a totally unexpected way, I had an encounter with the living God. After I returned to the cabin, I immediately sat behind my word processor and typed in the occurrence that I had experienced. I didn't want to lose it or exaggerate it. Since this experience will have special meaning to most of us who are called to leadership, I am sharing it with you. I have only done some minor editing so that it can apply to you in your walk with the Lord.

Crossing the Creek, No Turning Back

I had an amazing spiritual experience this morning. I went out for a jog, and I took a road that I am totally unfamiliar with. After jogging for awhile through the countryside and then through a winding dirt road that took me through the woods, I came upon a creek (small river) that crossed the road, and my jogging came to a screeching halt. I was ready to turn around and go back when I heard a still, small voice within me tell me, "Take your shoes off and cross over the creek barefooted." I sensed that I was on holy ground.

In my flesh, I really didn't want to cross. I am not accustomed to going barefooted and the thought of taking off my shoes and crossing the creek and getting my feet all muddy and perhaps step on a sharp stone really wasn't my cup of tea. But I continued to hear this voice deep within my spirit telling me to take off my shoes and cross over.

I then began to understand with my spirit man. The Lord was asking me to take a step of obedience and faith and cross over the creek barefooted (which was a sign of humility). This was not just a natural creek, but also it had deep spiritual significance for my life and for DOVE Christian Fellowship. The Lord was asking me to cross the creek in faith and in humility, and allow the water to wash away all of the hurts, expectations, fears, insecurities, and ways of doing things from the past so that the Lord could teach me fresh and anew for the future.

I obeyed the prompting of the Holy Spirit and took my shoes off and slowly walked across the "river" to the other side. It was a holy experience. A cleansing from the past took place deep in my spirit.

As I took this step of obedience, I sensed that others who are called to serve with me in leadership will need to do the same thing spiritually—walk across the creek in humility and allow the water of the Holy Spirit to wash them clean of many of the hurts, mind-sets, and expectations of the past. The Lord has called us from the wilderness to the promised land of Canaan. We must forget what is behind and press on to what the Lord has for us in the future.

I asked the Lord if this means that we should change our name as a church. The response that I got was, "Your name didn't change when you crossed the creek so why should the name change?" The change is in the spirit. It would be possible to change the name and nothing would change in the spirit. The Lord's desire, as I understand it, is for us to move on from a Moses mentality to a Joshua mentality.

Moses and the people of God walked "in a circle" for forty years. Joshua had a clear mandate from the Lord to go into the promised land and take it back from the enemy. Moses majored on maintenance, while Joshua led an army! Each member of the army had clear areas to champion and to conquer; however, they were all committed to walk together to fulfill the purposes of the Lord.

I am called (along with those who are willing to cross the creek with me) to take the people of God into the promised land. In reality, in the same way that Joshua fulfilled the original vision that was given to Moses at the burning bush, I believe that the Lord is calling me to fulfill the original vision that He gave me years ago when He asked me if I am willing to be involved with the underground church, and then a few years later when the Lord asked me to start something new. I know I am committed to fulfilling the original vision the Lord gave to me in the late '70s and in January of 1980.

Beware of the Dogs

I walked for awhile barefooted and then sat down to put my shoes and socks back on. As I continued to walk down this road that was totally unknown to me, I had a few other significant experiences. First of all, the road took me into unknown territory. Less than a half mile up the road I had to walk past a mobile home. There were two dogs barking at me as I walked past, one on either side of the road. The one was really close to the road and was a ferocious looking beast. At first, fear flashed within me, but I knew that I was making the right decision. I just smiled and spoke gently to the barking dog and walked on by. It hit me as I walked by that there was certainly nothing to fear. Both of these dogs were chained and could bark and make all of the noise that they wanted, but they still could not touch me or harm me in any way.

I believe as I and others take this step of faith and each of us individually in the spirit make a decision to cross the creek, there will be some "dogs barking" (words spoken, perhaps harshly, against us), but it doesn't matter, the enemy cannot touch us. God knows our hearts, and He will vindicate.

As I continued to walk, it was as if a whole new world were opening up before me. The fields were beautiful, and it was a sheer delight to walk along these country roads. I had a clear sense that I was walking in the right direction, but in reality, it was a real step of faith. I had never been here before in my life. I believe that this is clearly symbolic of the future. We will walk in the direction that we believe the Lord wants us to walk, and yet have to totally trust the precious Holy Spirit for direction. I believe there will be a tremendous sense of peace as we trust the Holy Spirit in this way.

The Joy of Building

The next thing that happened, I see as extremely significant. I passed an old Methodist church building. A brand new building was being built on the back side of the same property. There were all kinds of people hustling and bustling around, working together on this project. The roof and the aluminum siding were on. What was so amazing to me was that the workers were women, teens, and men all joyfully working together to fulfill a common purpose—build the new church building. Along with the men, I saw women and a teenage girl with a nail bag tied around their waists. I felt the excitement and the joy and the expectancy within the people as I walked by. I again sensed the still, small voice within me saying, "This is what it is going to be like as you have crossed the creek, and others cross the creek with you. There shall be much joy."

As these people were working together to build a physical building, the Lord is calling together a company of His people to work together to build His spiritual building. And in the same way that these workers were inexperienced in the eyes of the world, the Lord will use those who may appear to be *inexperienced in the eyes of the church to build His spiritual house. These workers were also using new lumber to build this building, and the Lord is going to require of us to use new lumber (new Christians) in the building of this spiritual house.*

I believe that we will experience a working together to fulfill the Lord's purposes that will be much greater than anything that we have ever experienced. I have no desire to go back to the "good old days" because, in reality, they really weren't that good anyway.

I am in no way minimizing the wonderful things that the Lord has done in past years. However, I find that whenever I begin to be nostalgic, I have a tendency to forget the negative things that have happened in the past and only concentrate on the positive. I believe that the Lord has wonderful plans for those who are willing to forget the past and press on to what the Lord has in the future.

And sure enough, the road that I traveled by faith brought me back to the cabin. I will never forget this experience. It was worth taking off for the three month sabbatical just for this spiritual experience. May the Lord Jesus Christ be praised!

I now had renewed faith and vitality to press forward in the calling God had given to me years ago—to be involved in building the underground church through small groups. I had crossed the river.

It's All By His Grace

But by the grace of God I am what I am, and His grace toward me was not in vain; but I labored more abundantly than they all, yet not I, but the grace of God which was with me (I Corinthians 15:10).

It has been a privilege for many of us to see firsthand these spiritual principles at work in five continents of the world during the past few years. But we need to do more than live by principles. We really need Jesus and His grace to see any lasting fruit from our own feeble efforts.

The key to what happens in each cell group is that nothing happens except by the grace of God. We are totally dependent upon His grace. God's grace is "His free unearned favor on the undeserving and the ill deserving." It is also "the power and the desire to do God's will." And the Lord has given us this grace through faith in His son Jesus Christ!

The responsibility to make something happen is God's. You and I simply need to be obedient. Plant your seeds in faith. Expect them to grow. But in reality, it is not your responsibility to make them grow. We co-labor with God to build for His glory.

We can do all things through Christ which strengthens us! (Philippians 4:13). Scriptures tell us that He gives more grace to the humble (James 4:6). It is Christ who dwells in us who gives us the will and the ability to do what pleases Him! (Philippians 2:13).

If you believe that the Lord may be calling you to labor with Him to build His church according to the underground principles that are outlined in this book, you will probably have to cross your own river. After you cross, there is no turning back. But then, who wants to go back to the wilderness? Let's march like Joshua, through the river, with a confidence that the Lord is saving the best wine for last. And He is waiting for you and me to prepare the wineskins so that He can pour out His Spirit, from house to house, city to city, and nation to nation. Let's take a step of faith together today.

CHAPTER 16

Giving the Church Away

Update! In 1996, DOVE Christian Fellowship International (DCFI) transitioned to an apostolic network of cell-based churches. The next two chapters chronicle how DCFI gave the church away in order to continue to plant cells and churches throughout the world. And the story continues...

At DOVE Christian Fellowship International, we have often made the statement, "the only thing that is constant is change"! The good thing about change is it often provides an opportunity for us to learn to trust the sovereignty of God more fully.

In the last several years, since *House to House* was first published, DCFI has continued to wholeheartedly pursue the vision and calling God has given us—to build the underground church (cell groups) around the world. During the past few years, it became clearer to us that in order for DCFI to accomplish what God originally had in mind, we needed to adjust our church government and be willing to "give the church away."

How do you "give a church away"?

When our oldest daughter, Katrina, was married this past year, we realized we had spent 21 years giving her our time, resources, love, encouragement, and finances. Then, we became aware we had made this investment in her to give her away to a young man who would be her husband. We had trained her to give her away.

Our Lord is calling us to train and invest in His people to

give them away! We need to live with the expectation that many of the believers presently serving in cell groups and churches will eventually have their own families (new cell groups and new churches they will plant). We need to be constantly training people to give them away.

We, at DCFI, realized we could not really do this effectively within our existing church structure. God wanted us to trust His sovereignty as He again nudged us toward change. We recognized the Lord had called us to be an international family of churches and ministries, an "apostolic movement," and we began to take steps to make the transition.

What is an Apostolic Movement?

This "apostolic movement" is comprised of people with various gifts that share common vision, values, goals, and a commitment to plant and nurture churches and ministries worldwide. An "apostolic movement" has God-given authority and responsibility to serve, train, equip, release and protect the people, ministries, and churches throughout the movement, all the while advancing the kingdom of God.

We see our "apostolic movement" as a family of churches and ministries with a common focus: a mandate from God to labor together to plant and establish cell churches and cell-based church-planting movements throughout the world.

As a cell-based, church-planting movement, we were always intent on training a new generation of church planters and leaders. So, a family of self-governing churches better suited our goal of mobilizing and empowering God's people. In this way, everyone—individuals, families, cells and congregations—can fulfill His purposes at the grass roots level.

We believe every cell group should have a God-given vision to plant new cells. We also believe every congregation should have a God-given vision to plant new churches. This gives all of us a chance to spread our wings and fly!

The Transition to a New Model

On January 1, 1996, after more than two years of preparing for transition, our cell-based church in Pennsylvania became eight, self-governed churches, each with its own elder-ship team. We formed an Apostolic Council to give spiritual oversight to DCFI, and I was asked to serve as its International Director.

We also realized our need for input from outside the DCFI family to provide the Apostolic Council with advice, counsel and accountability. So a team of "recognized spiritual advisors" (spiritual fathers in the church-at-large) was formed to provide accountability for the Apostolic Council.

The newly formed Apostolic Council gave each church eldership team the option of becoming a part of the DCFI family of churches and ministries or connecting to another part of the body of Christ. Each of these eight churches expressed a desire to work together with us to plant churches throughout the world and became a part of the DCFI family. The majority of the overseas church plants also became a part of the DCFI family of churches and ministries.

We decided to call these churches "partner churches." We became a movement of churches partnering together to fulfill the Great Commission of reaching the lost and making disciples locally, nationally and internationally.

This transition was not easy for many of us. I enjoyed being the "Senior Pastor" of a mega-church with the security it seemed to bring. Those of us on the leadership team and staff of DCFI had to walk in a new level of faith in the Lord, as the finances we had received week after week from the tithes of one large, local church were now given to each self-governing, cell-based church. In some ways, it was almost like starting over. Yet, since the transition, we have experienced the faithful provision of the Lord as we have walked in obedience to Him.

We have found the apostolic movement provides a safe environment for growth and reproduction. This new model emphasizes leading by relationship and influence rather than hands-on management and control from the top.

The Apostolic Council members are responsible to give clear vision and direction to the entire movement as they spend time in prayer, the Word, giving training, oversight, and mentoring local church leadership. By developing supportive relationships with local church elders, they influence the elders but do not have direct authority to make local decisions.

In each church, it is the senior elder and the eldership team who lead their congregation by hands-on management. They have leadership gifts to equip believers to do the work of ministry in cell groups within a congregation. The eldership team is responsible for direction, protection, and correction in that local body. They make decisions for their cell-based church with the input and general affirmation of the cell leaders and the congregation.

The Apostolic Council gives basic oversight, but each local church eldership team is responsible to train the believers in their church. In this way, each church has its own identity while embracing the same basic values as the rest of the DCFI family.

One of these churches, in Manheim, Pennsylvania, became a self-governed cell-based church with their own eldership. This church, DOVE Christian Fellowship Manheim, has already been involved in planting a new cell-based church in the nation of Scotland, a new cell-based church in Lancaster, Pennsylvania (a city about 12 miles away), and a new cell-based church in Red Lion, Pennsylvania, all within three years!

The multiplication process continues as each church gives away the people the Lord has given to them. Otherwise, we become a bottleneck to the future leadership the Lord is raising up among us. In a business corporation, we say a person has reached a *glass ceiling* when he or she can go no further in the corporation. They may have the potential and talent, but there is nowhere for them to advance. The multiplication process in a cell-based church affords limitless potential. People are constantly given the opportunity to be trained and then released (or given away) to start new churches.

Broadening Our Focus

Although DCFI has always had a call to plant new churches, we had been encouraged by various leaders to make it possible for other cell-based churches to become a part of the DOVE family. A few years ago, the Lord spoke to my heart a message that has since broadened our focus. He spoke through His still, small voice, "I have many orphans in my body, and I am calling you to adopt some of my orphans." I knew He was calling us to open our hearts to cell-based churches (sharing vision and values like ours) which are without spiritual oversight and apostolic protection.

Now, in addition to church planting and multiplication, the Lord has given us a process for churches called to become a part of the DCFI family. After going through a one year "engagement" period, churches with similar values and vision are becoming partner churches with the DCFI family. Ron Myer, who has served with me as a cell leader, pastor and elder for many years, serves on the DCFI Apostolic Council and oversees a team of leaders who serve churches that are considering partnering with the DCFI family.

Partnering Together

Our transition from one church to eight churches allowed the old structure to die so we could experience the new—a network of cell-based churches partnering together. At the time of this printing, there are currently 80 cell-based congregations either in the engagement period or partnering with the DCFI family from the nations of Barbados, Bulgaria, Canada, Croatia, Kenya, New Zealand, Scotland, Uganda, and the United States. The Lord has taken us on an amazing ride during the past few years.

Our desire is to see congregations of cell groups clustered together in the same areas so leaders can easily meet as regional presbyteries for prayer and mutual encouragement and to find ways to be more effective in building His kingdom together. Senior elders of DCFI churches in Pennsylvania have the blessing of meeting together each month for prayer and mutual encouragement. An Apostolic Council member also meets every month individually with each senior elder.

Each DCFI partner church is governed by a team of elders and consists of believers committed to one another in cell groups. Each cell and local church has its own identity while being interdependent with the rest of the DCFI family.

188 / House to House

Spiritual Parenting ²⁶

An important philosophy at DCFI is releasing each believer in ministry. We call this "spiritual parenting." Local church leadership is trained and encouraged to delegate authority and responsibility for ministry to the believers within the cell groups. As elders empower cell leaders to freely serve God's people by giving them responsibility and authority, the Lord releases every believer to be a minister.

We encourage church leaders to take the risk of empowering and releasing cell leaders to minister to others by: performing water baptisms, serving communion, praying for the sick, giving premarital and post-marital counseling, discipling new believers, reaching out in evangelism, and providing missions opportunities.

A major aspect of cell ministry is preparing and training future spiritual fathers and mothers. I will never forget the experience of having our first baby. I had faithfully attended prenatal classes with LaVerne where I learned how to coach. But when the contractions started, reality hit me. We were going to have a baby! I just didn't feel like I was ready; I was too young. We had never done this before. I felt like telling LaVerne, "Couldn't you just put it on hold for a few months until we are ready for this?" But, waiting was not an option. She was ready to give birth, and our brand new baby girl was born.

It really felt strange being a "papa." We had never been down this road before. But somehow, with the faithful advice of trusted family and friends, it all worked out. That was twenty-two years ago. When this "baby" girl got married, we gave her away. She had gone from being a baby, to a teenager, to an adult. And now, she will have the opportunity to be a parent and prepare the next generation.

When it comes to spiritual parenting, many potential spiritual parents go through the same emotions and fears. "How could God ever use me to be a spiritual parent? What if I can't do it properly? Am I really ready for this?" But as they are encouraged to take a step of faith and obedience, they begin to experience the joy of becoming a spiritual father or mother. They have the satisfaction of training and releasing others for eternity.

Only a dysfunctional parent will try to hang on to his children and use them to fulfill his own vision. Healthy parents expect their children to leave their home to start their own families. Healthy spiritual parents must think the same way. This generation of Christian leaders are called to "give away" many of the believers in their churches to start their own spiritual families—new cell groups and new churches.

According to the Bible, there are three different types of people in our churches: spiritual children, young men, and fathers. I John 2: 12-13 tells us, "I write to you **little children,** because your sins are forgiven you for His name's sake. I write to you **fathers [and mothers],** because you have known him who is from the beginning. I write to you **young men [and women],** because you have overcome the wicked one." Let's look at these three types of people and how they can be prepared and trained to become spiritual parents.

Spiritual Babies

There are many spiritual babies (new Christians) in the church today, with few spiritual fathers and mothers available to disciple them. But the larger problem seems to be the many spiritual babies who have never grown up, many of them unaware they are still infants. Their spiritual chronological age may be twenty, thirty, forty or fifty years old, but they remain on "the milk." They make a fuss when they don't get their own way, complain about not being fed, and have not yet taken spiritual responsibility to train the next generation.

Spiritual Young Men and Women

Spiritual young men, according to the Bible, have the Word of God abiding in them and have overcome the wicked one. They have learned to feed on the Word for themselves in order to overcome the devil. But they have not yet become spiritual fathers.

When I was a child, I thought my father knew everything. When I became an adolescent, I felt there were a few things he didn't know. By the time I was in my mid teens, in my youthful arrogance, I just figured my father was still living in the stone ages. But when I became a father, I was amazed at how much my father had learned during the past few years! The truth was, in my becoming a father, my perspective changed. In the same way, having spiritual children also changes our perspective.

One of the greatest catalysts to maturity as a Christian is to become a spiritual father or mother. Many of the problems that surface in churches today are the product of: (1) spiritual young men and women who are full of the Word of God but have not had the experience of becoming spiritual parents, and (2) church leaders who have not released and encouraged the spiritual young men and women within their church to have their own spiritual children.

Spiritual Fathers and Mothers

So how does a young man or woman become a spiritual parent? He or she could quote the entire book of Leviticus from memory and still not be a spiritual parent. Let's review what Paul said to the Corinthian church in I Corinthians 4:15-16.

> "For though you might have ten thousand instructors in Christ, yet you do not have many fathers; for in Christ Jesus I have begotten you through the gospel. Therefore I urge you, imitate me."

The only way for a young man or woman to become a spiritual parent is to have children. One can have children either by adoption (becoming a spiritual father to someone who is already a believer but needs to be discipled) or by natural birth (becoming a spiritual father to someone we have personally led to Christ) and committing ourselves to helping them grow. The cell group provides an ideal opportunity for everyone to experience a spiritual family and eventually become a spiritual parent themselves. The purpose of cell multiplication is to see new parents take responsibility for a new spiritual family (cell).

In the early 1970s, LaVerne and I, with a team of young people, began to develop Paul-Timothy relationships with new Christians. I would meet with a few young men each week for Bible study, prayer and to try to answer their questions about life. LaVerne did the same with young women. Watching them grow from spiritual babies, to young men and women, to spiritual parents has brought great joy to our lives. It has also caused great growth in our personal spiritual lives.

There is a tremendous need for spiritual parents in the church today. I can still hear the desperation in the voice of a dynamic young leader in New Zealand who opened his heart to me a few years ago. "I need a father. Where are the spiritual fathers today?" Jesus took twelve men and became a spiritual father to them for three and a half years. He knew that Christianity was caught more than taught. He ministered to the multitudes, but most of His time was spent with these few men. His disciples changed the world. By our Lord's example, we can do the same.

You Can be a Spiritual Parent!

Perhaps you feel you have already tried to be a spiritual parent, but failed. Trust God for grace to start again. Someone once asked Mother Teresa what she does when she gets discouraged. "I don't get discouraged," she said. "God has called me to be faithful, not successful."

Maybe you never had a spiritual father or mother. You can give someone else something you never had by being their spiritual parent. You do not need to be perfect, just faithful and obedient. If you and I wait until we think we are ready to be the perfect parent, it will never happen.

Are you expecting the believers in your church and cell group to become spiritual fathers or mothers? If not, you need to change your way of thinking. Many will become cell leaders, fulfilling their roles as spiritual parents in the coming days. And many present cell leaders will become future elders, church planters, and apostolic leaders. They are presently experiencing "on-the-job training." Remember, we train them to give them away!

Cell leaders are called by the Lord to become spiritual parents to believers in cell groups. Elders and pastors become spiritual parents to cell leaders. Apostolic leaders become spiritual parents to elders and pastors. The Lord is restoring spiritual parents to His church in these days.

CHAPTER 17

PREPARING FOR
THE HARVEST

California redwood trees are known to be some of the largest trees in the world. The secret of their ability to stand tall is not in their deep root system. The secret is in the fact that the roots of the trees are interconnected with the roots of the trees growing around them. They are interdependent. Each one needs the others.

Our desire is to see churches planted in clusters in the same geographical area so leaders can easily meet as regional presbyteries for prayer and mutual encouragement, and find ways to be more effective in building His kingdom together. Like the redwoods, they become interdependent upon one another.

The Blessing of Teamwork

Senior elders of DOVE churches in Pennsylvania have the blessing of meeting together each month for prayer and mutual encouragement. An Apostolic Council member also is committed to meet at least once each month individually with each senior elder.

The Lord, by His grace, has given us an extraordinary support team at DCFI. This team consists of the Apostolic Council, a team of Fivefold Translocal Ministers, and various ministries like the Stewardship Council handling financial matters. All are committed to resource the leadership and believers in DCFI partner churches and serve the greater body of Christ. These various ministries offer leadership training and ministry development on many levels. For example, Steve

Prokopchak, who serves on the DCFI Resource Team, travels regularly to churches throughout the United States and the world training cell leaders and elders to give both premarital and post-marital counseling to young couples in their churches.

A few years ago, we recognized the need to more effectively train cell-based church leaders and church planters. Recognizing this need resulted in starting the *House to House Cell-Based Church Planting and Leadership School*. This 150-session leadership training school is producing lasting fruit by giving practical Scriptural leadership tools for both present and future cell leaders, elders and church planters.

Since many who wanted to receive this training could not move to Pennsylvania to participate in the school, the Lord helped us to produce a video correspondence school in three modules. This training is now being utilized by churches from different denominations and movements throughout the world. Brian Sauder, a member of the DCFI Apostolic Council and the director of the *Cell-Based Church Planting and Leadership School* "flies the flag" for cell-based church planting.

Prayer is the Key to the Harvest

An important twenty-four hour Prayer Ministry includes a team of "prayer generals" who recruit, train, and encourage a team of "prayer warriors" responsible to cover segments of time each week to pray for the entire DCFI family. These "Prayer Generals" and "prayer warriors" are scattered throughout the nations of the world.

Resourcing the Body of Christ

What the Lord has given to us, He has called us to openly share with the rest of the body of Christ. It will take all the existing churches and many new churches working together to see the harvest reaped. A team of experienced leaders from DCFI travel all over North America training cell leaders and church leaders throughout the body of Christ in practical cell-based ministry through "Helping You Build Seminars." Cell Ministry Conferences, Youth Cell Conferences, and Church Planting Clinics are hosted at various times throughout the year to serve and resource the broader body of Christ. Publications tools and resources from *House to House Publications* are used by churches of many denominations and movements throughout the United States, Canada, and the world.

The Apostolic Council and leadership from DCFI partner churches worldwide meet together each March for an annual International Leadership Conference for the purpose of mutual encouragement, leadership training, relationship building, and to receive a common vision from the Lord. The Lord has called us to work as a team together—with a shared vision, shared values, a shared procedure, and to build together by relationship. In order for the DCFI family of churches and ministries to be effective in laboring together, our procedure is written in a publication called the "DCFI Leadership Handbook."

House Church Networks [27]

Like our early beginnings, we are again sensing that the harvest is upon us. The Lord, like a great magnet, is drawing people into His kingdom. Since new wineskins eventually get old, many who have been believers for years are becoming dissatisfied with life as it is in their present church structures. God's people are again thirsting for new wine and new wineskins. The Lord is renewing and refreshing and reviving thousands of His people all over the world. He is requiring us to provide new wineskins for the new wine, as He brings in His harvest.

We are already seeing evidence of some of these new kinds of wineskins such as "house churches" sprouting up throughout the nations. China, especially, has the most strategically organized house church movement in the world. House churches often meet in homes like cell groups but they are very different. Whereas cell groups usually function as a complementary ministry to the larger Sunday church meeting, a house church is the church itself—a complete little church with its own elders.

Many effective house churches are cell-based. For example, a new house church begins as one group, but wise leaders often train more leaders within the group to lead small satellite cell groups. So then, one house church may be comprised of several small cell groups. In a geographical area, house churches often network to stay accountable and share resources.

We believe that as we continue to reach the lost in our generation, many new kinds of churches are needed. Traditional community churches and mega-churches will coexist and network with the newer house churches, and God will bless all three! For more on house churches, read Larry Kreider's book, *House Church Networks, A Church for a New Generation* (see page 213).

Empowering the Next Generation

Each generation is different and has different needs and preferences. We are committed to empowering, releasing, and supporting the next generation as they fulfill their particular call in God.

As Elisha received a double portion of the spirit that was on Elijah, our desire is to see our spiritual children far exceed us in developing their spiritual gifts and church leadership. Believers will be called to various areas of leadership: cell group leadership, local church leadership, fivefold ministry, and apostolic leadership.

The long-term goal of DCFI is to establish many apostolic councils in various regions of the world. Ibrahim Omondi, from Nairobi, Kenya, gives oversight to a new apostolic leadership team made up of African leaders who are responsible for oversight of DCFI churches in Africa. Eventually, the leadership for the DCFI movement will be a DCFI International Apostolic Council, whose members will include apostolic leaders from many nations. This International Apostolic Council will be responsible for the spiritual oversight and mentoring of apostolic leaders and apostolic councils located throughout the world.

As an international family of churches and ministries, we are called to keep actively involved in what the Lord is doing in the world and participate in the present expressions of His anointing. We desire to empower, train, and release God's people at the grass roots level to fulfill His purposes. After all, it happened two thousand years ago in the book of Acts. Let's join together as the body of Christ, and in obedience to our God, trust Him to experience the book of Acts again!

Appendix A

As we explained in Chapter 11, it's important for a church to have a vision, a mission statement and a plan. This is the vision, mission statement and plan of DCFI:

Our Vision

To build a relationship with Jesus, with one another, and to reach the world from house to house, city to city, nation to nation.

Our Mission

To exalt Jesus Christ as Lord, obey His Word, and encourage and equip each believer for the work of ministry. We are called to build the church from house to house, city to city, and nation to nation through small groups. This "underground church" is built through prayer, reaching the lost, and making disciples. Our mission includes reaching adults, youth and children for Christ. We are also called to church planting, proclaiming the Gospel through media, and building unity in the body of Christ. As a spiritual army, we will cooperate with the church that Jesus is building throughout the world in fulfilling the Great Commission.

Our Plan

By the grace of God we will accomplish our mission by:
1. **Strengthening** our faith through the daily meditation of the Word of God and **developing** an intimate relationship with Jesus.
2. **Committing** ourselves to other believers in a small group.
3. **Praying** to the Lord of the harvest to send out laborers into the harvest fields: locally, nationally and internationally.
4. **Encouraging** every believer to be involved in prayer, reaching the lost, and making disciples.
5. **Helping** each believer to learn to serve and discover the gifts and callings within his life.
6. **Teaching** the Word of God with power and authority in a way that is practical and applicable to everyday life.

7. **Releasing** apostles, prophets, evangelists, pastors and teachers to equip the saints for the work of ministry and to build up the body of Christ.

8. **Training** and **equipping** leadership in home cell groups and congregations to minister to others and to plant new churches.

9. **Planting** and **multiplying** home cell groups and congregations locally, nationally and internationally.

10. **Sending** laborers to the harvest field: house to house, city to city, and nation to nation.

11. **Caring** for, **loving, healing,** and **restoring** those who are wounded and need deliverance, healing, and restoration.

12. **Promoting** unity by **supporting, networking** together and **laboring** with other churches and ministries locally, nationally and internationally.

13. **Mobilizing** and **challenging** adults, youth, and children to be radically committed laborers for the harvest.

14. **Utilizing** all forms of media to proclaim the gospel.

15. **Resourcing** each believer through the ministry of helps, administration and communication.

16. **Ministering** to the poor and needy.

17. **Encouraging** each child, young person and adult to be a worshipper.

18. **Giving** of tithes, offerings, material possessions and our time to the building of the kingdom.

19. **Exemplifying** a life-style of accountability, integrity, and purity in every level of leadership and throughout every area of church life.

20. **Supporting** and **encouraging** the spiritual leaders that the Lord raises up among us.

21. **Edifying** one another daily through encouragement and speaking the truth in love.

22. **Celebrating** Jesus as we come together in various locations to worship together, pray together, and receive the Word of God together.

23. **Partnering** with believers within the DCFI family of churches who are meeting from house to house and city to city to reach the world together.

24. **Receiving** the filling of the Holy Spirit to minister Jesus to our generation through the demonstration of His supernatural power and gifts.

DOVE Christian Fellowship International Values of the Kingdom

1. Our Foundations: Knowing Christ and Living by the Word of God

We believe that the basis of the Christian faith is to know God through repentance for sin, receiving Jesus Christ as Lord, building an intimate relationship with Him, and being conformed into His image. God has declared us righteous through faith in Jesus Christ (John 1:12, John 17:3, Rom. 8:29, II Cor. 5:21).

All values for the DOVE Christian Fellowship International family must be rooted in the scriptures (II Tim. 3:16-17, II Tim. 2:15).

DOVE is an acronym: Declaring Our Victory Emmanuel (God with us).

2. Complete Dependence on the Holy Spirit

We recognize that we desperately need the person and power of the Holy Spirit to minister effectively to our generation. Changed lives are not the product of men's wisdom, but in the demonstration of the power of the Holy Spirit as modeled in the New Testament church (I Cor. 2:2-5, John 15:5).

All decisions need to be made by listening to the Holy Spirit as we make prayer a priority and learn to be worshippers (II Cor. 13:14, John 4:23-24).

We recognize that we do not wrestle against flesh and blood, but against demonic forces. Jesus Christ is our Lord, our Savior, our Healer and our Deliverer (Eph. 6:12, I John 3:8).

3. The Great Commission: Prayer, Evangelism, Discipleship, and Church Planting

We are committed to helping fulfill the Great Commission through prayer and fasting, evangelism, discipleship, and church planting locally, nationally, and internationally (Matt. 28:19-20, Matt. 6:5-18, Acts 1:8).

We are called to support others who are called as co-laborers, as churches are planted throughout the world. The Great

Commission can only be fulfilled through church planting (I Cor. 3:6-9, Acts 14:21-23).

We are also called to proclaim the gospel through the arts, publications, and the media and will continue to believe God to raise up other resources and ministries to assist us in building the church (I Cor. 9:19-22).

4. The Covenant of Marriage and Training our Children to Know Christ

It is our belief that marriage and family are instituted by God, and healthy, stable families are essential for the church to be effective in fulfilling its mission. Parents are called by God to walk in the character of Christ and train their children in the nurture and loving discipline of the Lord Christ (Mark 10:6-8, Eph. 5:22-6:4).

The Lord is calling His people to walk in the fear of the Lord and in a biblical standard of holiness and purity. Marriage covenants are ordained by God and need to be honored and kept (Prov. 16:6, Mark 10:9, I Thess. 4:3-8, I Cor. 6:18-20).

5. Spiritual Families, Spiritual Parenting, and God Connecting the Generations

Believing that our God is turning the hearts of the fathers and mothers to the sons and daughters in our day, we are committed to spiritual parenting on every level of church and ministry life (Mal. 4:5-6, I Cor. 4:15-17).

Participation in a cell group is a fundamental commitment to the DCFI family. The cell group is a small group of believers and/or families who are committed to one another and to reaching others for Christ. We believe the Lord desires to raise up spiritual families in many levels including cells, congregations, apostolic movements and the kingdom of God (I Cor. 12:18, Eph. 4:16).

We believe each spiritual family needs to share common values, vision, goals, and a commitment to build together, with the need to receive ongoing training in these areas (Ps. 133, II Pet. 1:12,13, II Tim. 2:2).

6. Multiplication and Spiritual Reproduction

Multiplication should be expected and encouraged in every area of church life. Cell groups should multiply into new cells and churches should multiply into new churches. Church planting should be a long term goal of every congregation (Acts 9:31, Mark 4:20).

The DCFI family of churches will be made up of many new regional families of churches as apostolic fathers and mothers are released in the nations of the world (Acts 11:19-30, Acts 13-15).

7. God's Kingdom is Built through Relationships and Family

Serving others and building trust and relationships should be experienced in every area of church life. We believe the best place to begin to serve and experience trust and relationship is in the cell group (Acts 2:42-47, Eph. 4:16, Gal. 5:13).

We are joined together primarily by God-given family relationships, not by organization, hierarchy, or bureaucracy (I Peter 2:5).

8. Every Believer is Both a Priest and a Minister

According to the scriptures, every Christian is a priest who needs to hear from the Lord personally (Rev. 1:5-6).

Every believer is called of God to minister to others and needs to be equipped for this work with the home as a center for ministry. Fivefold ministers are the Lord's gifts to His church. He uses fivefold persons to help equip each believer to become an effective minister in order to build up the body of Christ (I Pet. 4:9, Eph. 4:11-12).

We need to be constantly handing the work of ministry over to those we are serving so they can fulfill their call from the Lord (Titus 1:5, I Tim 4:12-14).

We are committed to reaching, training and releasing young people as co-laborers for the harvest, as the young and the old labor together (Acts 2:17, Jer. 31:13).

9. Servant Leadership

We believe every sphere of leadership needs to include a clear servant-leader called by God and a team who is called to walk with him. The leader has the anointing and responsibility to discern the mind of the Lord that is expressed through the leadership team (Num. 27:16, I Peter 5:1-4).

Leaders are called to listen to what the Lord is saying through those whom they serve as they model servant-leadership. They are called to walk in humility, integrity, in the fruit of the Spirit, and in the fear of the Lord (Acts 6:2-6, Acts 15, Matt. 20:26, Gal. 5:22-23).

We believe God raises up both apostolic overseers and partner church elders to direct, protect, correct and discipline the church. These leaders must model the biblical qualifications for leadership (Acts 15, Acts 6:1-4, I Tim. 3, Titus 1).

Those with other spiritual gifts including administrative gifts (ministry of helps) need to be released to fulfill the Lord's vision on each level of church life (I Cor. 12).

In every area of church life we believe we need to submit to those who rule over us in the Lord and esteem them highly in love for their work's sake (Heb. 13:17, I Thess. 5:12-13).

10. Biblical Prosperity, Tithes, Offerings and Financial Integrity

Biblical prosperity is God's plan to help fulfill the Great Commission. The principle of the tithe is part of God's plan to honor and provide substance for those He has placed over us in spiritual authority. Those who are over us in the Lord are responsible for the proper distribution of the tithes and offerings (III John 2, Matt. 23:23, Heb. 7:4-7, Mal. 3:8-11, Acts 11:29-30).

We believe in generously giving offerings to support ministries, churches, and individuals both inside and outside the DCFI family, and emphasize giving to people as a priority. We encourage individuals, cells, congregations, and ministries to support fivefold ministers and missionaries in both prayer and finances (II Cor. 8:1-7, Gal. 6:6, Phil. 4:15-17).

We believe that every area of ministry and church life should be responsible financially and accountable to those giving them oversight in order to maintain a high standard of integrity. Spiritual leaders receiving a salary from the church should not set their own salary level (Gal. 6:5, Rom. 15:14, I Thess. 5:22).

11. Reaching the Unreached and Helping the Poor and Needy

Jesus instructs us to take the Gospel to the ends of the earth to those who have never heard. Our mission is to reach the unreached areas of the world with the Gospel of Jesus Christ and through church planting. Together we can join with the body of Christ to reach the unreached (Matt. 24:14, Acts 1:8, II Cor. 10:15-16).

We are also called to help the poor and needy, those in prison, orphans and widows. This includes our reaching out to the poor locally, nationally and internationally. When we help the poor, both materially and spiritually, we are lending to the Lord. He pays great interest on our investment! (Deut. 14:28, 29; Deut. 26: 10-12, Matt. 25:31-46, James 1:27, Prov. 19:17).

12. Building the Kingdom Together with the Rest of the Body of Christ

Our focus is on the kingdom of God, recognizing our cell group, our local church, and DCFI is just one small part of God's kingdom. We are called to link together with other groups in the body of Christ and pursue unity in His church as we reach the world together (Matt. 6:33, Eph. 4:1-6, John 17, Ps. 133).

We believe in utilizing and sharing the resources of people and materials the Lord has blessed us with. This includes the fivefold ministry, missions, leadership training, and other resources the Lord has entrusted to us (I Cor. 12, Acts 2:44-45).

Our unifying focus is on Christ, His Word and the Great Commission, and we believe we should not be distracted by minor differences (Romans 14:5).

We subscribe to the Lausanne Covenant as our basic statement of faith and Christian values. The scriptures serve as a light to guide us, and the Lausanne Covenant along with these values unite us as Partner churches as we walk together in the grace of God (Matt. 28:19-20, Amos 3:3, I Cor. 1:10, I Cor. 15:10).

NOTES

Chapter 1

1 Harold Eberle, *The Complete Wineskin*, (Helena, Montana, 1989), pp. 144, 145.

2 Jim Petersen, *Church Without Walls*, (Colorado Springs, Colorado: NavPress, 1992), pp. 148, 149.

Chapter 3

3 James H. Rutz, *The Open Church*, (Auburn, Maine: The SeedSowers, 1992), p. 47.

4 T.L. Osborne, *Soulwinning Out Where the Sinners Are*, (Tulsa, Oklahoma: Harrison House, 1980), pp. 35, 36, 37.

5 Howard A. Synder, *The Radical Wesley*, (Downers Grove, Illinois: Inter-Varsity Press, 1980), pp. 53, 54, 55, 56, 57, 63.

6 Terry Taylor, *Perspectives*, January 1993.

7 Ralph Neighbour, *The Seven Last Words of the Church*, (Grand Rapids, Michigan: Zondervan Publishing House, 1973), p. 164.

Chapter 6

8 Dr. Paul Yonggi Cho, *Successful Home Cell Groups*, (Plainfield, New Jersey: Logos International, 1981), pp. 90, 93, 94.

Chapter 7

9 Francis Anfuso, "Two Question Test" booklet, P. O. Box 17728, South Lake Tahoe, CA 95706.

Chapter 8

10 Ralph W. Neighbour, Jr., *Where Do We Go From Here?*, (Houston, Texas: Touch Publications, Inc., 1990), p. 247.

11 Some of the insights about "embracing our missionaries" are from Terry Pfautz, former Mission Director of DCFI.

12 This section is written by Mel Sensenig, former Director of *World Net*, a onetime international student ministry of DCFI.

13 Ralph W. Neighbour, Jr., *Where Do We Go From Here?*, (Houston, Texas: Touch Publications, Inc., 1990), p. 204.

14 Larry Kreider, *Biblical Foundation Series*, (Available through House to House Publications: Ephrata, PA). Web site: www.dcfi.org

Chapter 9

15 Ralph Neighbour, Jr., *Where Do We Go From Here?*, (Houston, Texas: Touch Publications, Inc., 1990), p.437.
16 Don and Gail Gunstone, *Home Fellowship Meetings, Creative Ideas*, (Portland, Oregon: Bible Temple Publishing, 1986). Ralph W. Neighbour, Jr., *Shepherd's Guidebook*, (Houston, Texas: Touch Publications).

Chapter 10

17 *Emotional Dependency* and *Codependency* sections (pp. 129-130) written by Steve Prokopchak who oversees the Counseling Resource Department of DOVE Christian Fellowship International.
18 More on emotional dependency, (Steve Prokopchak, *Recognizing Emotional Dependency*), as well as other helpful booklets for cell leaders, available through DOVE Christian Fellowship International, Ephrata, Pennsylvania: House to House Publications. Web site: www.dcfi.org
19 Leanne Payne, *Restoring The Christian Soul Through Healing Prayer*, (Wheaton, Illinois: Crossway Books, 1991).

Chapter 11

20 "Dynamic Preaching," *Net Results Magazine*, March 1991, p. 30.

Chapter 12

21 Bill Scheidler, *The New Testament Church and Its Ministries*, (Portland, Oregon: Bible Temple Publishing), p. 88.
22 Kevin J. Conner, *The Church In the New Testament*, (Portland, Oregon: Bible Temple Publishing, 1989), p. 110.

Chapter 14

23 Rick Joyner, *The Harvest*, (Charlotte, North Carolina: Morning Star Publications, Inc., 1989), p. 46.
24 Carl George, *Prepare Your Church For the Future*, (Tarrytown, New York: Fleming H. Revell Company, 1991), p. 51.
25 Kevin J. Conner, *Today's Prophets*, (Portland, Oregon: Bible Temple Publishing), p. 20.

Chapter 16

[26] For more about spiritual parenting, read: Larry Kreider, *The Cry for Spiritual Fathers & Mothers*, (Ephrata, PA: House to House Publications, 2001). See page 213 for ordering information.

Chapter 17

[27] For more about house churches, read: Larry Kreider, *House Church Networks, A Church for a New Generation*, (Ephrata, PA: House to House Publications, 2001). See page 213 for ordering information.

INDEX

A

apostles, 23,29,147-153,158,172-176
assistant cell leaders, 39,42,49,60,63-66,123
apostolic
 council, 185,191,193,195-196
 leader/overseer, 156
 ministry, 151-152,174,185
 movement, 184

B-C

biblical foundations, 39-40
cells
 discipling relationships, 15,22,24,65-66,98
 homogeneous, 94-96
 new believers in, 97-98
cell groups
 biblical vision for, 19
 birthdays and anniversaries, 69
 commissionings, 123
 dissolving the group, 122-123
 divisiveness in, 133
 flexibility, 10,37,116,135,142,172-176
 finances of, 68
 future vision, 26-27
 house to house principle, 20-21
 members of the body, 38-39
 money for missions, 27
 multiplication, 119-121,186,190
 nontraditional setup, 25-26
 number of people in, 122
 primary focus of, 85
 priorities: prayer, evangelism,
  discipleship, 13-16
 social activities, 69
 structure, 3,5,26,28,36-37,139,172
cell leader
 calling of, 42
 commitment
  "commitment card,"143
  willing to change, 141-143
  to church, 137-138
  to goals, 139-140
  to Jesus, 137
  to vision of church, 138-139
 confidentiality, 134-135
 dealing with problems, 128
 delegate, 127-128

 leadership limited, 62
 qualifications, 41
  accountable, 51-53
  clear testimony, 43-44
  encouraged to tithe, 50-51
  enthusiastic, 47-48
  full of faith, 44-45
  have a pastor's heart, 66-67
  in unity with spouse, 49-50
  person God calls, 53-54
  not a novice, 48-49
  personable, 47
  recognize leadership, 48
  set an example, 67-68
  support local church, 45-46
 responsibilities, 57-60
  be trained, 63-65
  confirming new leaders, 65
  encourage, not control, 60-61
  pray, 57-60
  train assistants, 63
cell meetings
 baby dedication, 118-119
 flexible and creative, 116-117
 location or relationship, 96-96
 call people by name, 114
 choosing a home, 108
 communion, 118
 gifts of Spirit, 112-113
 maintaining order, 111
 meeting time and format, 108-111
 ministering to children, 115-116
 not a mini-celebration, 105
 snacks and food, 116
 teachings, 106-107
 water baptism, 117
 worship leaders, 114-115
cell members
 emotional dependency, 129-132
 in times of change/crisis, 125-127
church
 adopting, 186
 give it away, 183
 grass roots movement, 171-173
 it happened in a home, 169-170
 planting, 8,10,184
 three kinds of, 170-171
church discipline, 133-134
church planting, 8,10,184

D

deacons, 66,157,164-165
discipleship, 22,25,85-86,98-103
DOVE Christian Fellowship Int'l
   churches planted, 10
   cell group structure, 10
   getting back on track, 9-10
   its history, 1-11
   learn from mistakes,10-11
   its start, 6
   mission statement, 197
   need for clear leadership, 6-7
   need for flexible wineskins, 3
   our terminology, 34-35
   partnering, 187
   plan, 197-198
   underground church, 3-5
   update,183-196
   vision, 19,197
   vision frustrated, 9

E-F

early church, 21-22
elders,29,35,52,147-148,152-157,173-176
Elijah principle, 83-84
evangelism, 14-15,85-94,164
   International students, 93-94
fivefold ministry, 162-164
flexible wineskins, 3
future vision, 173-176

G-H-I-J

grass roots movement, 171-173
harvest, 193-196
head and shoulders, 155
holy buildings, 159,165-167
holy men, 160-162
   pastor myth, 162
hospitality, 77-80
house church networks, x,195
house to house principle, 20-21
Icthus Fellowship, London, 156
Jethro principle, 27-30

L

leadership, 7
   God-appointed, 154-155
   apostle/elders unity, 154
   head and shoulders, 155
   decision-making, 156
living stones, 22-23

M-N-O-P

members of body, 38-39
Meserete Kristos Church, 102
Methodist revival, 24-25
missions, 92-93
multiplication process, 119-121,186
net mending, 35
oikos principle, 86-89
partner churches, 185
Paul-Timothy relationships, 190
prayer, 13,83,99,101,105,108,140,
167,170,194

R-S-T

release people, 29,187-191
revival, 35,99,140,165,166,169
section leader, 36,60,124
senior elders and overseers
   decision-making, 151
   hands-on management, 185
   their role, 34
servanthood, 69
   Jesus taught, 70
   leadership without it, 71
   sowing and reaping, 72
   hirelings or shepherds, 73
servant-leadership, 69
   motivation of, 74
serving
   motivation of, 74
   by building relationships, 77
   by sharing hospitality, 75
   through encouragement, 78
   those no longer active in cell, 79
spiritual families, 31-33,187-191
spiritual fathers/mothers, 95,187-191
teamwork, 193-194
tradition, 25
transition, 184-185

U

underground church, 3
unity, 140

W

wineskins, 2
   new houses/rooms, 195
   new vessels, 97

Growing Healthy Cell Groups Seminar

This dynamic seminar offers field-tested training to help you grow effective cell groups. For pastors and cell leaders.

Youth Cells Ministry Seminar

Learn the values behind youth cells so cell ministry does not become just another program at your church.
For adult and teen leaders!

Spiritual Fathering & Mothering Seminar

Practical preparation for believers who want to have and become spiritual parents. Includes a *Spiritual Parenting Manual* and the book *The Cry For Spiritual Fathers & Mothers*.

Church Planting Clinic

A clinic designed to help you formulate a successful strategy for cell-based church planting. For those involved in church planting and those considering it.

Counseling Basics Seminar for Small Group Leaders

This seminar takes you through the basics of counseling, specifically for small group ministry.
Includes a comprehensive manual.

Fivefold Ministry Seminar

A seminar designed to release healthy, effective fivefold ministry in the local church.

Affordably priced!

Call for complete brochures

1-800-848-5892

**For dates, locations and details check our Web site:
www.dcfi.org   email: dcfi@dcfi.org**